SIMPLY DELICIOUS

D0189826

Darina Allen

SIMPLY DELICIOUS

Published for Radio Telefís Éireann
by
Gill and Macmillan

Published in Ireland by
Gill and Macmillan Ltd
Goldenbridge
Dublin 8
with associated companies in
Auckland, Delhi, Gaborone, Hamburg, Harare,
Hong Kong, Johannesburg, Kuala Lumpur, Lagos, London,
Manzini, Melbourne, Mexico City, Nairobi,
New York, Singapore, Tokyo
© Darina Allen, 1989
0 7171 1687 5
Photographs by Peter Harding
Food styling by Rory O'Connell
Design by Peter Larrigan
Print origination in Ireland by Irish Typesetting and Publishing Ltd, Galway
Printed in Spain by Graficas Estella, Navarra

All rights reserved. No part of this publication may be copied,
reproduced or transmitted in any form or by any means,
without permission of the publishers.

*For my Simply Delicious husband
Tim*

Contents

The items marked with an asterisk denote recipes which are demonstrated on RTE's *Simply Delicious* television series.

Foreword

It is twenty years since I came to Ballymaloe, fresh from hotel school in Dublin. I was the first 'outsider' to come into Myrtle Allen's kitchen and she taught me herself. Her approach to cooking and the kind of food she served in her restaurant instantly appealed to me — real food with true flavours and simple sauces.

No imported foie gras or truffles here; we cooked the wonderful fresh food produced around us. Fresh vegetables, fruit and herbs from the garden, fish from Ballycotton and superb beef and lamb from local pastures. When rosy-cheeked local children came to the door with blackberries, damsons or field mushrooms these were included in the menu which was written each day.

Myrtle recognised, nurtured and encouraged my enthusiasm, and I settled in; in fact I became one of the family by the simple expedient of marrying her eldest son! Now her philosophy is also mine and through the years she and my father-in-law, Ivan, have encouraged me, first to start giving classes and eventually in 1983 to open the Ballymaloe Cookery School. There I teach people not only from Ireland but from all over the world how to cook on the principles that Myrtle taught me.

I teach them how to find the very best raw ingredients because they are the essential basis of good cooking. I encourage them to cook food when it is in season because of course it is at its best and cheapest then.

Gardening is my other great love and fresh herbs are an indispensable part of our cooking. I grow my own and I encourage you to do the same, even if it's only possible in pots or in a window box. Fresh herbs, more than anything else, can add magic to your cooking.

Many of the recipes I've chosen to share with you are recipes that Myrtle Allen taught me years ago. I've picked them not only because they are simple to cook and taste delicious, but because they illustrate many important basic techniques; so once you have mastered these recipes you can do many other variations on the same theme.

I love cooking myself and I always feel sad when people tell me that they don't enjoy cooking, because it seems to me that with this one skill we can give so much pleasure to our family and our friends. More than anything else I want to take the mystique out of cooking and show everyone how easy it is to cook simply delicious food.

Glossary

De-glaze: After meat has been sautéed or roasted, the pan or roasting dish is de-greased and then a liquid is poured into the pan to dissolve the coagulated and caramelised pan juices. This is the basis of many sauces and gravies. The liquid could be water, stock or alcohol, e.g. wine or brandy.

De-grease: To remove surplus fat from a liquid or a pan, either by pouring off or by skimming the surface with a spoon.

Grill pan: A heavy cast-iron pan, with a ridged bottom, either round or rectangular. The ridges mark the food attractively while keeping the meat or fish from direct contact with the fat. A heavy pan gives a good even heat.

Macerate: To soak fruit in syrup or other liquid so that it will absorb flavour and in some cases become more tender.

Palette knife: A useful but not essential piece of kitchen equipment, it is a blunt knife with a rounded tip, and a flexible blade useful for spreading meringue etc.

Reduce: To boil down a liquid to concentrate the flavour. This is a very important technique in sauce-making.

Roux: Many of the sauces in this book call for roux. Roux is a basic liaison of butter and flour which is used as a thickening agent. Use equal quantities. Melt the butter and stir in the flour. Cook on a low heat for 2 minutes, stirring occasionally.

Roux can be stored in a covered bowl and used as required. It will keep for approx. 2 weeks in a refrigerator. 90 g/3 ozs/$\frac{1}{4}$ cup of roux will thicken 600 ml/1 pint/$2\frac{1}{2}$ cups of liquid. The liquid should be boiling as you whisk in the roux, otherwise it won't thicken properly.

There are three types of roux: white, blond and brown. If you melt the butter and just stir in the flour, that makes a white roux. If you cook it for 2 minutes on a gentle heat, it becomes a blond roux, perfect for pale sauces. If however you continue to cook the roux until it becomes golden brown, then you have a brown roux more suitable for gravies and dark sauces. We use blond roux as an all-purpose roux, using 450 g/1 lb each of butter and flour at a time.

Roux is tremendously useful to have ready prepared in your kitchen.

Sweat: To cook vegetables in a little fat or oil over a gentle heat in a covered saucepan, until they are almost soft but not coloured.

Tomato concassé: A term used to describe a small dice of peeled, ripe tomato flesh. Concassé may be added to a sauce or used as a garnish.

Soups and Starters

I feel that starters are a very important part of a meal because they can really set the mood, so aim to serve small portions of something that tastes delicious and looks tempting.

Both Cruditées with Garlic Mayonnaise and Carrot and Apple Salad with Honey and Vinegar Dressing certainly fit that description and the latter has the added advantages that it only takes a few minutes to make, the ingredients are cheap and you would probably have them in the house anyway. We serve it as a starter but it is also delicious as an accompanying salad with cold meats, particularly ham or pork.

The Old-Fashioned Salad is just the sort of thing you would get for tea, perhaps with a slice of ham, if you went to visit your granny in the country on a Sunday. It is delicious served with this dressing which Myrtle Allen got from a Quaker lady called Lydia Strangman who used to live in our house years ago, hence the name Lydia's Dressing. Nowhere is the importance of having superb flavourful ingredients more evident than in this simple salad: it can be glorious or dull, depending on the quality of your ingredients.

The Timbales of Smoked Salmon will steal the show. This is a very stylish starter but again it only tastes as it should when made with really good Smoked Irish Salmon. I mention this point particularly because there is a lot of Smoked Salmon of disgraceful quality on the market. Read your label carefully and make sure that you are actually buying Smoked *Irish* Salmon. *Irish Smoked* Salmon could and often does mean poor quality Canadian or Norwegian frozen Salmon which is smoked in this country and sold at 'bargain prices'. There is no such thing as a 'bargain' in Smoked Salmon: really good quality Smoked Salmon costs a lot to produce, so save your money for a special occasion and buy the best. Grated horseradish gives a delicious perk to the Timbales recipe, but if you can't find fresh horseradish, use a little extra lemon juice instead.

I decided to include Salmon Pâté and Salmon Rillettes because they are both excellent recipes which use left-overs of fresh or smoked salmon. In fact they are so good you could make them specially!

The Pink Grapefruit Sorbet is tremendously versatile. It makes a deliciously refreshing starter but can also be served before the main course in a meal of several courses; it would then have the effect of cleansing the palate: in other words, you would feel less full and be able to tuck into several more courses quite happily — and have room for pudding as well!

I have also included some of my favourite soups in this section, cheap and cheerful soups that are wonderfully warming for a family supper or equally delicious to start a dinner party. I made Purée of Onion Soup with Thyme Leaves on the programme because I felt that most people would have onions and potatoes in the house at any time and so they could use this recipe. These soups are all made on our basic soup formula which works with almost any vegetable you have. You can use just one main vegetable or a mixture as in Lettuce, Cucumber and Mint. Remember to make more soup than you need because it takes about the same time; it will keep in the refrigerator for several days or you can freeze some for an emergency.

Cruditées with Garlic Mayonnaise*

Cruditées with Garlic Mayonnaise is one of my favourite starters. It fulfills all my criteria for a first course: small helpings of very crisp vegetables with a good garlicky home-made mayonnaise. The plates of Cruditées look tempting, taste delicious and, provided you keep the helpings small, are not too filling. Better still, it's actually good for you—so you can feel very virtuous instead of feeling pangs of guilt!

Another great plus for this recipe I've discovered is that children love Cruditées. They even love Garlic Mayonnaise provided they don't hear some grown up saying how much they dislike garlic, and you can feel happy to see your children polishing off plates of raw vegetables for their supper, really quick to prepare and full of wonderful vitamins and minerals.

Cruditées are a perfect first course for Winter or Summer, but to be really delicious one must choose very crisp and fresh vegetables. Cut the vegetables into bite-sized bits so they can be picked up easily. You don't need knives and forks because they are usually eaten with fingers.

Use as many of the following vegetables as are in season:

very fresh button mushrooms, quartered
tomatoes quartered, or left whole with the calyx on if they are freshly picked
purple sprouting broccoli, broken (not cut) into florettes
calabrese (green sprouting broccoli), broken into florettes
cauliflower, broken into florettes
French beans or mange tout
baby carrots, or larger carrots cut into sticks 5 cm/2 inches long approx.
cucumber, cut into sticks 5 cm/2 inches long approx.
tiny spring onions, trimmed
red cabbage, cut into strips
celery, cut into sticks 5 cm/2 inches long approx.
chicory, in leaves
red, green or yellow pepper, cut into strips 5 cm/2 inches long approx., seeds removed
very fresh Brussels sprouts, cut into halves or quarters
whole radishes, with green tops left on
parsley, finely chopped
thyme, finely chopped
chives, finely chopped
sprigs of watercress

A typical plate of Cruditées might include the following: 4 sticks of carrot, 2 or 3 sticks of red and green pepper, 2 or 3 sticks of celery, 2 or 3 sticks of cucumber, 1 mushroom cut in quarters, 1 whole radish with a little green leaf left on, 1 tiny tomato or 2 quarters, 1 Brussels sprout cut in quarters, and a little pile of chopped fresh herbs.

Wash and prepare the vegetables. Arrange on individual white side plates in contrasting colours, with a little bowl of Garlic Mayonnaise in the centre. Alternatively, do a large dish or basket for the centre of the table. Arrange little heaps of each vegetable in contrasting colours. Put a bowl of Garlic Mayonnaise in the centre and then guests can help themselves.

Instead of serving the Garlic Mayonnaise in a bowl one could make an edible container by cutting a slice off the top of a tomato and hollowing out the seeds. Alternatively, cut a 4 cm/1½ inch round of cucumber and hollow out the centre with a melon baller or a teaspoon. Then fill or pipe the Garlic Mayonnaise into the tomato or cucumber. Arrange in the centre of the plate of Cruditées.

Note: All vegetables *must* be raw.

Mayonnaise

Mayonnaise is what we call a 'mother sauce' in culinary jargon. In fact it is the 'mother' of all the cold emulsion sauces, so once you can make Mayonnaise you can make any of the daughter sauces by just adding some extra ingredients.

I know it's very tempting to reach for the jar of 'well-known brand', but most people don't seem to be aware that Mayonnaise can be made, even with a hand whisk, in under five minutes; and if you use a food processor the technique is still the same but it's made in just a couple of minutes. The great secret is to have all your ingredients at room temperature and to drip the oil very slowly into the egg yolks at the beginning. The quality of your Mayonnaise will depend totally on the quality of your egg yolks, oil and vinegar and it's perfectly possible to make a bland Mayonnaise if you use poor quality ingredients.

2 egg yolks, free-range
¼ teasp. salt
pinch of English mustard *or* ¼ teasp. French mustard
15 ml/1 tablesp. white wine vinegar

250 ml/8 fl ozs/1 cup oil (sunflower, arachide *or* olive oil, *or* a mixture)

Serve with cold cooked meats, fowl, fish, eggs and vegetables.

Clockwise from right
Salad of Carrot and Apple with Honey and Vinegar Dressing; Timbales of Smoked Salmon with Cucumber and Fennel Salad; Cruditées with Garlic Mayonnaise; Purée of Onion Soup with Thyme Leaves; (*centre*) Grapefruit Sorbet

Cruditées with Garlic Mayonnaise

Grapefruit Sorbet

Purée of Onion Soup with Thyme Leaves

Salad of Carrot and Apple with Honey and Vinegar Dressing

Put the egg yolks into a bowl with the mustard, salt and 1 dessert-spoon of wine vinegar (keep the whites to make meringues). Put the oil into a measure. Take a whisk in one hand and the oil in the other and drip the oil onto the egg yolks, drop by drop, whisking at the same time. Within a minute you will notice that the mixture is beginning to thicken. When this happens you can add the oil a little faster, but don't get too cheeky or it will suddenly curdle because the egg yolks can only absorb the oil at a certain pace. When all the oil has been added, whisk in the remaining vinegar. Taste and add a little more seasoning if necessary.

If the Mayonnaise curdles it will suddenly become quite thin, and, if left sitting, the oil will start to float to the top of the sauce. If this happens you can quite easily rectify the situation by putting another egg yolk or 1–2 tablespoons of boiling water into a clean bowl, then whisk in the curdled Mayonnaise, a half teaspoon at a time until it emulsifies again.

Garlic Mayonnaise

Ingredients as above and	2 teasp. chopped parsley
1–4 cloves of garlic depending on size	

Crush the garlic and add to the egg yolks just as you start to make the Mayonnaise. Finally add the chopped parsley and taste for seasoning.

Note: Here is a tip for crushing garlic. Put the whole clove of garlic on a board, preferably one that is reserved for garlic and onions. Tap the clove with the flat blade of a chopping knife, to break the skin. Remove the skin and discard. Then sprinkle a few grains of salt onto the clove. Again using the flat blade of the knife, keep pressing the tip of the knife down onto the garlic to form a paste. The salt provides friction and ensures the clove won't shoot off the board!

Salad of Carrot and Apple with Honey and Vinegar Dressing*

Serves 6

This delicious salad is very quick to make but shouldn't be prepared more than half an hour ahead, as the apple will discolour.

225 g/8 ozs/2 cups grated carrot	285 g/10 ozs/2 cups grated dessert apple, e.g. Cox's Orange Pippin if available

2 good teasp. pure Irish honey

1 tablesp./4 American teasp.
white wine vinegar

Garnish
a few leaves of lettuce
sprigs of watercress *or* parsley

chive flowers if you have them

Dissolve the honey in the wine vinegar. Mix the grated carrot and apple together and toss in the sweet and sour dressing. Taste and add a bit more honey or vinegar as required, depending on the sweetness of the apples.

Take 6 white side plates. Arrange a few small lettuce leaves on each plate and divide the salad between the plates. Garnish with sprigs of watercress or flat parsley and sprinkle with chive flowers if you have some.

Note: Carrot and Apple Salad may also be served as an accompanying salad and goes particularly well with cold ham, bacon or pork.

Old-fashioned Salad with Lydia's Dressing*

Serves 4

This simple old-fashioned salad is one of my absolute favourites. It can be quite delicious when it's made with a crisp lettuce, good home-grown Irish tomatoes and cucumbers, free-range eggs and home-preserved beetroot. If on the other hand you make it with pale battery eggs, watery tomatoes, tired lettuce and cucumber and—worst of all—vinegary beetroot from a jar, you'll wonder why you bothered!

We serve this traditional salad in Ballymaloe as a starter, with an old-fashioned salad dressing which would have been popular before the days of mayonnaise.

1 butterhead lettuce (the
ordinary lettuce that one can
buy everywhere)
2 hard-boiled eggs, quartered
2–4 tomatoes, quartered
16 thin slices of cucumber

4 slices of home-preserved
beetroot (see below)
4 tiny scallions *or* spring onions
2–4 sliced radishes
chopped parsley

Lydia's Dressing
2 hard-boiled eggs
1 level teasp./1 American teasp.
dry mustard
pinch of salt
15 g/1 tablesp./4 American teasp.
soft brown sugar

15 ml/1 tablesp./4 American
teasp. brown malt vinegar
56–130 ml/2–4 fl ozs/$\frac{1}{4}$–$\frac{1}{2}$ cup
cream

Hard-boil the eggs for the Salad and the Dressing: bring a small saucepan of water to the boil, gently slide in the eggs, boil for 10 minutes (12 if they are very fresh), strain off the hot water and cover with cold water. Peel when cold.

Wash and dry the lettuce and scallions.

Next make the Dressing. Cut 2 eggs in half, sieve the yolks into a bowl, add the sugar, a pinch of salt and the mustard. Blend in the vinegar and cream. Chop the egg whites and add some to the sauce. Keep the rest to scatter over the salad. Cover the Dressing until needed.

To assemble the salads: Arrange a few lettuce leaves on each of 4 plates. Scatter a few quartered tomatoes and 2 hard-boiled egg quarters, a few slices of cucumber and 1 radish or 2 slices of beetroot on each plate. Garnish with spring onion and watercress, scatter the remaining chopped egg white (from the Dressing) over the Salad and some chopped parsley.

Put a tiny bowl of Lydia's Dressing in the centre of each plate and serve immediately while the salad is crisp and before the beetroot starts to run. Alternatively, the Dressing may be served from one large bowl.

Timbales of Smoked Salmon with Cucumber and Fennel Salad*

Serves 6

6 thin slices of smoked salmon

Smoked Salmon and Trout Pâté
125 g/4 ozs smoked salmon trimmings *or*
75 g/3 ozs smoked trout and 25 g/1 oz smoked salmon trimmings
30 g/1 oz unsalted butter

150 ml/5 fl ozs cream
1 tablesp. freshly-grated horseradish (optional)
lemon juice
salt and freshly-ground pepper

Cucumber and Fennel Salad
$\frac{1}{3}$ of a fresh cucumber

Vinaigrette
5 ml/1 tablesp. wine vinegar
42 ml/3 tablesp. sunflower oil

pinch each of mustard, salt, freshly-ground pepper and sugar
$\frac{1}{2}$ teasp. freshly-chopped fennel

Garnish
sprigs of chervil and fennel   little dice of fresh tomato flesh
                                                  (tomato concassé)

6 moulds (5 cm/2 inches diameter, 2.5 cm/1 inch deep, $2\frac{1}{2}$ fl ozs
   capacity)

A food processor is essential for this recipe, to achieve a really smooth filling.

Blend the smoked salmon and trout trimmings with the unsalted butter in a food processor, add grated horseradish and cream, and lemon juice to taste. Check seasoning and do not over process or the mixture will curdle.

Line the moulds with cling film. Put a slice of smoked salmon into each mould. Fill the moulds with the mousse, fold the ends of the smoked salmon over the mousse to cover. Cover with cling film and refrigerate for at least one hour.

Next make the vinaigrette by whisking the oil and vinegar together in a bowl for a few seconds. Season to taste with salt, freshly-ground pepper, sugar and a pinch of mustard. Slice the cucumber very finely by hand or on a mandolin, toss the cucumber slices in 3 tablespoons of the vinaigrette and add the very finely-chopped fennel.

To assemble: Arrange the cucumber slices in an overlapping circle on a large side plate. Place a timbale of salmon in the centre of the cucumber circle and glaze it with a little of the surplus vinaigrette. Garnish with sprigs of fresh chervil or fennel. Finally, a dessertspoon of tomato concassé or 2 cherry tomatoes peeled and halved can be used to make an attractive garnish on each plate.

Salmon Pâté with Fennel

Serves 6–8

This little pâté is a delicious way of using up left-over cold salmon.

110 g/4 ozs/1 cup cooked salmon, $\frac{1}{4}$ teasp. finely-snipped fennel
   free of skin and bone $\frac{1}{2}$ teasp. lemon juice
55–85 g/2–3 ozs/4–6 tablesp. $\frac{1}{2}$ clove of garlic, crushed to a
   softened butter   paste

Blend all the ingredients in a food processor or just simply in a bowl, taste and add more lemon juice if necessary.

Fill into a bowl or little pots, put a sprig of fennel on top of each pot. Cover with a thin layer of clarified butter (see page 37). Chill in the refrigerator. Serve within 3 days.

This pâté can also be piped in rosettes onto 5 mm/$\frac{1}{4}$ inch thick slices of cucumber and served as a starter or as part of a hors-d'oeuvre or buffet.

Rillettes of Fresh and Smoked Salmon

Serves 8

The texture of this pâté should resemble that of pork rillettes, where the meat is torn into shreds rather than blended.

340 g/$\frac{3}{4}$ lb/2$\frac{1}{2}$ cups freshly-cooked
  salmon
340 g/$\frac{3}{4}$ lb/2 cups smoked salmon
340 g/12 ozs/1$\frac{1}{2}$ cups softened
  butter

salt and freshly ground pepper
pinch of nutmeg
lemon juice to taste

For cooking the Smoked Salmon
30 g/1 oz/$\frac{1}{4}$ stick butter
28 ml/$\frac{1}{2}$ fl oz/2 American tablesp.
  water

Melt 30 g/1 oz butter in a low saucepan, add the smoked salmon and 1 tablespoon of water. Cover and cook for 3–4 minutes or until it no longer looks opaque. Allow it to get quite cold.

Cream the butter in a bowl. With two forks, shred the fresh and smoked salmon and mix well together. Add to the soft butter still using a fork (do *not* use a food processor). Season with salt and freshly-ground pepper and nutmeg. Taste and add lemon juice as necessary, and some freshly-chopped fennel if you have it.

Serve in individual pots or in a pottery terrine. Cover with a layer of clarified butter (see page 37). Serve with hot toast or hot crusty white bread. Salmon Rillettes will keep perfectly in the refrigerator for 5 or 6 days provided they are sealed with clarified butter.

Pink Grapefruit Sorbet*

Serves 8

Sorbets are usually served at the end of a meal, but a grapefruit sorbet can be served at the beginning, in the middle, or at the end, so it is particularly versatile.

You may use ordinary yellow grapefruit, but this recipe is especially delicious if you can find pink grapefruit which are sweeter and have a pale pink juice. Pink grapefruit look very like ordinary ones although they sometimes have a pink blush and are always a bit more expensive. They are at their best between November and February when the flesh is very pink inside. If you are using ordinary grapefruit you will need to increase the sugar to about 300 g/$10\frac{1}{2}$ ozs.

1 L/$1\frac{3}{4}$ pints/35 fl ozs pink grapefruit juice (10 grapefruit approx.)	225 g/8 ozs/1 cup plus 1 tablesp. castor sugar approx. 1 egg white (optional)

Garnish

4 grapefruit cut into segments	fresh mint leaves

8 chilled white side plates

Squeeze the juice from the grapefruit into a bowl, dissolve the sugar by stirring it into the juice. Taste. The juice should taste rather too sweet to drink, because it will lose some of its sweetness in the freezing.

Make the sorbet in one of the following ways:

1. Pour into the drum of an ice-cream maker or sorbetière and freeze for 20–25 minutes. Scoop out and serve immediately or store in a covered bowl in the freezer until needed.

2. Pour the juice into a stainless steel or plastic container and put into the freezer or the freezing compartment of a refrigerator. After about 4 or 5 hours when the sorbet is semi-frozen, remove from the freezer and whisk until smooth; then return to the freezer. Whisk again when almost frozen and fold in one stiffly-beaten egg white. Keep in the freezer until needed.

3. If you have a food processor simply freeze the sorbet completely in a stainless steel or plastic bowl, then break into large pieces and whizz up in the food processor for a few seconds. Add one slightly-beaten egg white, whizz again for another few seconds, then return to the bowl and freeze again until needed.

To serve: Chill the plates in a refrigerator or freezer. Carefully segment the grapefruit by cutting off all the peel and pith first. Then with a stainless steel knife remove each segment from the membrane. Put 1 or 2 scoops of sorbet on each chilled plate, garnish with a few segments of pink grapefruit, put a little grapefruit juice over the segments and decorate with fresh mint leaves.

Purée of Onion Soup with Thyme Leaves*

Serves 6 approx.

45 g/1½ ozs/3 level tablesp. butter
450 g/1 lb/4 cups chopped onions
140 g/5 ozs/1 cup chopped
  potatoes
1 teasp. fresh thyme leaves
1.1 L/2 pints/5 cups home-made
  chicken stock

150 ml/¼ pint/generous ½ cup
  cream *or* cream and milk
  mixed, approx.
salt and freshly-ground pepper

Garnish
fresh thyme leaves and thyme *or*
  chive flowers

a little whipped cream (optional)

Peel and chop the onions and potatoes into small dice. Measure. Melt the butter in a heavy saucepan. As soon as it foams, add the onions and potatoes; stir until they are well coated with butter. Add the thyme leaves, season with salt and freshly-ground pepper, cover with a paper lid (to keep in the steam) and the saucepan lid, and sweat on a low heat for 10 minutes approx. The potatoes and onions should be soft but not coloured. Add the chicken stock, bring it to the boil and simmer until the potatoes are cooked, 5–8 minutes approx. Liquidise the soup and add a little cream or creamy milk. Taste and correct seasoning if necessary.

Serve in soup bowls or in a soup tureen garnished with a blob of whipped cream; sprinkle with thyme leaves and thyme or chive flowers.

Potato and Fresh Herb Soup

Serves 6

Most people would have potatoes and onions in the house even if their cupboards were otherwise bare, so one could make this 'simply delicious' soup at a moment's notice. While the vegetables are sweating, pop a few white soda scones into the oven and then you will have a nourishing meal.

55 g/2 ozs/4 tablesp. butter
110 g/4 ozs/1 cup diced onions
425 g/15 ozs/3 cups peeled diced
  potatoes
1 teasp./1 American teasp. salt
freshly-ground pepper

2–3 teasp. in total of the
  following: parsley, thyme,
  lemon balm and chives
1.2 L/2 pints/5 cups home-made
  chicken stock
130 ml/4 fl ozs/½ cup creamy milk

Melt the butter in a heavy saucepan. When it foams, add the potatoes and onions and toss them in the butter until well coated. Sprinkle with salt and pepper. Cover and sweat on a gentle heat for 10 minutes. Add the fresh herbs and stock and cook until the vegetables are soft. Purée the soup in a blender or food processor. Taste and adjust seasoning. Thin with creamy milk to the required consistency. Serve sprinkled with a few freshly-chopped herbs.

Lettuce, Cucumber and Mint Soup

Serves 6

40–55 g/1½–2ozs/¼–½ stick butter
110 g/4 ozs/1 cup diced onions
140 g/5 ozs/1 cup peeled diced potatoes
140 g/5 ozs/1 cup unpeeled diced cucumber
170 g/6 ozs/3 cups chopped lettuce leaves (without stalk)

salt and freshly-ground pepper
1.2 L/2 pints/5 cups home-made chicken stock
2 teasp./2 American teasp. freshly-chopped mint
36 g/4 tablesp./¼ cup cream (optional)

Melt the butter in a heavy saucepan. When it foams, add the potatoes and onions and turn them until well coated. Sprinkle with salt and freshly-ground pepper. Cover and sweat on a gentle heat for 10 minutes, until soft but not coloured. Add the cucumber and toss it in the butter. Add the stock, bring to the boil and cook until the potatoes, onions and cucumbers are completely cooked. Add the lettuce and boil *with the lid off* for about 4–5 minutes, until the lettuce is cooked. Do not overcook or the soup will lose its fresh green colour. Add the mint and cream if using, and liquidise. Taste and correct seasoning if necessary. Serve in warm bowls garnished with a blob of whipped cream and a little freshly-chopped mint.

Note: A few tips:
1. We use butterhead lettuce, outside leaves are perfect.
2. Light chicken stock should be used.
3. Fresh mint is more fragrant in Summer than in Winter, so it may be necessary to use more mint towards the end of the season.
4. If this soup is to be reheated, just bring it to the boil and serve immediately. Prolonged boiling will spoil the colour and taste.

Spring Cabbage Soup

Serves 6

Myrtle Allen puts this delicious soup on the menu in Ballymaloe several times during late Spring.

55 g/2 ozs/4 tablesp. butter
110 g/4 ozs/1 cup onions
140 g/5 ozs/1 cup chopped potatoes
210 g/7 ozs/3 cups chopped spring cabbage leaves (stalks removed)

1 L/35 fl ozs/5 cups light chicken stock
salt and freshly-ground pepper
56–130 ml/2–4 fl ozs/$\frac{1}{4}$–$\frac{1}{2}$ cup cream *or* creamy milk

Melt the butter in a heavy saucepan. When it foams, add the potatoes and onions and run them in the butter until well coated. Sprinkle with salt and freshly-ground pepper. Cover and sweat on a gentle heat for 10 minutes. Add the stock and boil until the potatoes are soft, then add the cabbage and *cook with the lid off* until the cabbage is cooked. Keep the lid off to retain the green colour. Do not overcook or the vegetables will lose both their fresh flavour and colour. Purée the soup in a liquidiser or blender, taste and adjust seasoning. Add 56–130 fl ozs/$\frac{1}{4}$–$\frac{1}{2}$ cup cream or creamy milk before serving.

If this soup is to be reheated, just bring it to the boil and serve. Prolonged boiling spoils the colour and flavour of green soups.

Fish

I'll never forget the first time I tasted really fresh fish, what a revelation! Tim who is now my husband cooked fresh plaice for me the first evening I came to Ballymaloe (the way to a girl's heart and all that!) My home was in the midlands in a little village called Cullohill in Co. Laois and when I was a child the bus travelling from Dublin to Cork dropped off fish every Thursday evening (ready for Friday!) at the shop in our village. It was usually whiting and smoked haddock and occasionally, when we were lucky, some plaice too. Plaice was our great favourite; we looked forward to it, dipped in seasoned flour and cooked in a little butter on the pan. I now know that the 'grand name' for that method is 'à la meunière', but then it was simply fried plaice. We thought it was delicious—but that was until I tasted *really* fresh plaice! It was incredible, I simply couldn't believe that it was the same fish. The sad thing is that there must be lots of people, particularly those living far from the sea, who still have never tasted really fresh fish and so can't quite appreciate what all the excitement is about! It's not until you taste fish just from the sea at the height of its season that you suddenly realise how exquisite it can be.

We now live only two miles from the little fishing village of Ballycotton so we get the most wonderful fish direct from the fishermen on the pier. Most of this fish is still caught in small boats and is landed every day, so the quality is superb. Fishing is not an easy life and fishermen often toil in wretched weather to bring us our catches of beautiful silver fish which makes me all the more determined to cook it as soon and as well as possible.

What a pity that many people don't eat fish on a regular basis. The situation is improving though, and Bord Iascaigh Mhara have done Trojan work over the years in making people aware of what a healthy food fish is, a fact borne out over and over again in independent studies. As a result, consumption of fish per capita has risen by 2 lbs in the last two years, but even so we still eat only 16 lbs of fish in comparison to 170 lbs of meat per head per year.

One problem certainly is distribution and availability of this very perishable food but enormous strides have been made in that direction. Many more fish shops have opened and several heroic people are travelling from the coast several times a week into the heart of the midlands with fish straight from the boats. Discover what day they come to your area, welcome them with open arms and buy while the fish is still fresh: they deserve your support and encouragement. Bring the fish home and cook it simply.

The recipes included in this section have been chosen not only because they are delicious but because they include techniques which can be used for many different kinds of fish. We pan-grill the mackerel and serve it with Maître d'Hôtel Butter but of course fillets or pieces of almost any fresh fish can be cooked in this way. Mackerel is particularly wonderful within hours of being caught — local fishermen always say that for perfection the sun shouldn't set on a mackerel before you eat it.

The technique we use for Baked Plaice or Sole with Herb Butter is one of our favourite ways of cooking flat fish. As a cooking method it has all the advantages because the fish is cooked on the bone for extra flavour, and with the skin on so it will stay moist. The skin is cut so you can peel it off easily and then spoon any sauce you choose over the fish, or if you just like to eat fish absolutely as it is for reasons of diet, then this is also a perfect way to cook it because it's totally fat free. We also cook brill or turbot this way.

I've included a recipe for cooking fish in foil for those who would like to cook a whole fish but don't have a fish kettle. Again many fish apart from salmon and sea mullet can be cooked in this way. Wild Irish salmon, poached gently in boiling salted water and served with a simple Hollandaise Sauce made from good Irish butter, can scarcely be bettered. When wild salmon is out of season one could use the farmed salmon which is being reared very successfully in Ireland and is getting better all the time. Bass, cod and the delicious and greatly under-estimated grey sea mullet are also wonderful served this way. Cod Baked with Cream and Bay-leaves is a master recipe which can be used for all kinds of round fish. You can ring the changes by using a different fresh herb or a mixture of herbs as in Sea Trout with Cream and Fresh Herbs.

Hollandaise Sauce makes any fish into a feast and, believe it or not, can be made well inside five minutes. It's a mother sauce so once you have mastered this technique you can make lots of 'daughter' sauces by just adding different garnishes, e.g. the Sauce Mousseline with turbot or brill, or the Cucumber and Tomato Hollandaise that we serve with monkfish.

15

Pan-grilled Mackerel with Maître d'Hôtel Butter*

Serves 4

8 fillets of very fresh mackerel
(allow 170 g/6 ozs fish for main
course, 85 g/3 ozs for a starter)

seasoned flour
small knob of butter

Maître d'Hôtel Butter
55 g/2 ozs/4 level tablesp. butter
4 teasp. finely-chopped parsley

juice of $\frac{1}{2}$ lemon

Garnish
segment of lemon

parsley

First make the Maître d'Hôtel Butter. Cream the butter, stir in the parsley and a few drops of lemon juice at a time. Roll into butter pats or form into a roll and wrap in greaseproof paper or tin foil, screwing each end so that it looks like a cracker. Refrigerate to harden.

Heat the grill pan. Dip the fish fillets in flour which has been seasoned with salt and freshly-ground pepper. Shake off the excess flour and then spread a little butter with a knife on the flesh side, as though you were buttering a slice of bread rather meanly. When the grill is quite hot but not smoking, place the fish fillets butter side down on the grill; the fish should sizzle as soon as they touch the pan. Turn down the heat slightly and let them cook for 4 or 5 minutes on that side before you turn them over. Continue to cook on the other side until crisp and golden. Serve on a hot plate with some slices of Maître d'Hôtel Butter and a segment of lemon.

Maître d'Hôtel Butter may be served directly on the fish, or if you have a pretty shell, place it at the side of the plate as a container for the butter. Garnish with parsley and a segment of lemon.

Note: Fillets of any small fish are delicious pan-grilled in this way. Fish under 900 g/2 lbs such as mackerel, herring and brown trout can also be grilled whole on the pan. Fish over 900 g/2 lbs can be filleted first and then cut across into portions. Large fish 1.8–2.7 kg/4–6 lbs can also be grilled whole. Cook them for 10–15 minutes approx. on each side and then put in a hot oven for another 15 minutes or so to finish cooking.

Sauté of Mackerel with Mushrooms and Herbs

Serves 4

4 very fresh mackerel
15 g/½ oz/1 tablesp. butter
4 teasp. finely-chopped fresh
  herbs: thyme, parsley, chives,
  fennel and lemon balm

125 g/4 ozs mushrooms
seasoned flour
1-2 cloves of garlic

Fillet the mackerel, wash, dry and dip in flour which has been seasoned with salt and freshly-ground pepper. Melt the butter in a pan large enough to take the fish in a single layer, and sauté the fish until golden on both sides. Meanwhile, chop the mushrooms and herbs finely and crush the garlic.

Remove the fish to a hot serving dish or 4 individual plates. Add the mushrooms and garlic to the pan. Cook for 2 or 3 minutes, add the fresh herbs and season with a little salt and freshly-ground pepper if necessary. Serve this mixture as a garnish down the centre of the fish.

Note: This mushroom, garlic and herb mixture is also delicious served with sauté chicken livers on toast, as a first course.

Poached Salmon with Hollandaise Sauce*

Serves 8

Most cookbooks you look up will tell you to poach salmon in a 'court-bouillon'. This is a mixture of wine and water with perhaps some sliced carrots, onion, peppercorns and a bouquet garni including a bay-leaf, but I feel very strongly that a beautiful salmon is at its best poached gently in just boiling salted water.

The proportion of salt to water is very important. We use 1 rounded tablespoon of salt to every 40 fl ozs/2 Imperial pints of water. Although the fish or piece of fish should be just covered with water, the aim is to use the minimum amount of water to preserve the maximum flavour, so therefore one should use a saucepan that will fit the fish exactly.

To Poach a Piece of Salmon

1.4–1.6 kg/3–3½ lbs centre-cut of
  fresh salmon
water

salt
Hollandaise Sauce (see below)

Garnish
fennel, chervil *or* parsley

8 segments of lemon

Choose a saucepan which will barely fit the piece of fish: an oval cast-iron saucepan is usually perfect. Half fill with measured salted water, bring to the boil, put in the piece of fish, cover, bring back to the boil and simmer gently for 20 minutes. Turn off the heat, allow to sit in the water and serve within 15–20 minutes.

If a small piece of fish is cooked in a large saucepan of water, much of the flavour will escape into the water, so for this reason we use the smallest saucepan possible. Needless to say we never poach a salmon cutlet because in that case one has the maximum surface exposed to the water and therefore maximum loss of flavour. A salmon cutlet is best dipped in a little seasoned flour and cooked slowly in a little butter on a pan, or alternatively pan-grilled with a little butter. Serve with a few pats of Maître d'Hôtel Butter (see page 16) and a wedge of lemon.

Hollandaise Sauce

Serves 4–6, depending on what it is to be served with

Hollandaise is the 'mother' of all the warm emulsion sauces. The version we use here is easy to make and quite delicious with fish. Like Mayonnaise it takes less than 5 minutes to make and transforms any fish into a 'feast'. Once the sauce is made it must be kept warm: the temperature should not go above 350°C/180°F or the sauce will curdle. A thermos flask can provide a simple solution on a small scale, otherwise put the Hollandaise Sauce into a delph or plastic bowl in a saucepan of hot but not simmering water. Hollandaise Sauce cannot be reheated absolutely successfully so it's best to make just the quantity you need. If however you have a little left over, use it to enrich sauces (see Cod with Cream and Bay-Leaves, page 26) or Duchesse Potato (page 27).

2 egg yolks, free-range	1 dessertsp. cold water
125 g/4 ozs butter cut into dice	1 teasp. lemon juice approx.

Serve with poached fish, eggs and vegetables.

Put the egg yolks in a heavy stainless steel saucepan on a low heat, or in a bowl over hot water. Add water and whisk thoroughly. Add the butter bit by bit, whisking all the time. As soon as one piece melts, add the next piece. The mixture will gradually thicken, but if it shows signs of becoming too thick or slightly 'scrambling', remove from the heat immediately and add a little cold water if necessary. Do not leave the pan or stop whisking until the sauce is made. Finally add the lemon juice to taste. If the sauce is slow to thicken it may be because you are excessively cautious and the heat is too low. Increase the heat slightly and continue to whisk until the sauce thickens to coating consistency.

It is important to remember that if you are making Hollandaise Sauce in a saucepan directly over the heat, it should be possible to put your hand on the side of the saucepan at any stage. If the saucepan feels too hot for your hand it is also too hot for the sauce.

Another good tip if you are making Hollandaise Sauce for the first time is to keep a bowl of cold water close by so you can plunge the bottom of the saucepan into it if it becomes too hot.

Keep the sauce warm until service either in a bowl over warm water, or in a thermos flask. Hollandaise Sauce should not be reheated. Left-over sauce may be used as an enrichment for cream sauces, or mashed potatoes, or to perk up a fish pie etc.

Poached Whole Salmon or Sea Trout to be served Hot or Cold

A whole poached salmon served hot or cold is always a dish for a very special occasion. Long gone are the days when the servants in great houses complained bitterly if they had to eat salmon more than twice a week!

If you want to poach a salmon or sea trout whole with the head and tail on, then you really need to have access to a 'fish kettle'. This is a long narrow saucepan which will hold a fish of 3.9–4 kg/$8\frac{1}{2}$ –9 lbs weight. Most people would not have a fish kettle in their houses, so if you want to keep the fish whole then the best solution would be to bake it in the oven wrapped in tin-foil (see below).

Alternatively, you could cut the salmon into three pieces, and cook them separately in the way I describe for cooking a piece of salmon on page 17. Later, you could arrange the salmon on a board or serving dish, skin it and do a cosmetic job with rosettes of mayonnaise and lots of fresh herbs.

A 3.4 kg/8 lbs salmon will feed 16 people very generously and it could quite easily be enough for 20. 125–140 g/$4\frac{1}{2}$ –5 ozs cooked salmon is generally plenty to allow per person as salmon is very rich. Use any left-over bits for Salmon Mousse or Salmon Rillettes.

Poached Whole Salmon or Sea Trout to be served Hot

1 whole salmon *or* sea trout
water

salt

Garnish
sprigs of fresh parsley, lemon
  balm and fennel
Hollandaise Sauce

a segment of lemon for each
  person

Special equipment
fish kettle

Clean and gut the salmon carefully; do not remove the head, tail or scales. Carefully measure the water and half fill the fish kettle, add 1 rounded tablespoon of salt to every 40 fl ozs/2 Imperial pints. Cover the fish kettle and bring the water to the boil. Add the salmon or sea trout and allow the water to come back to the boil. Cover and simmer gently for 20 minutes. Then turn off the heat and leave the salmon in the water until you wish to serve. It will keep hot for 20–30 minutes.

To serve: Carefully lift the whole fish out of the fish kettle and leave to drain on the rack for a few minutes. Then slide onto a large hot serving dish, preferably a beautiful long white china dish, but failing that, whatever it will fit on! Garnish with lots of parsley, lemon balm and fennel and 10–12 segments of lemon. I don't remove the skin until I am serving it at the table, then I peel it back gradually as I serve; however, if you prefer, remove the skin just at the last second before bringing it to the table. When you have served all the fish from the top, remove the bone as delicately as possible, put it aside and continue as before. Serve with Hollandaise Sauce (see page 18).

Poached Whole Salmon or Sea Trout to be served Cold

1 whole salmon *or* sea trout
water

salt

Garnish
crisp lettuce leaves
sprigs of watercress, lemon
  balm, fennel and fennel
  flowers if available

a segment of lemon for each
  person
home-made Mayonnaise

Special equipment
fish kettle

Clean and gut the salmon carefully; do not remove the head, tail or scales. Carefully measure the water and half fill the fish kettle, adding

Plaice fresh from Ballycotton Bay!

Poached Salmon with Cucumber Hollandaise

Ballymaloe Chicken Liver Pâté

A Green Salad with edible flowers

1 rounded tablespoon of salt to every 40 fl ozs/2 Imperial pints. Cover the fish kettle and bring the water to the boil. Add the salmon or sea trout and allow the water to come back to the boil. Simmer for just 2 minutes and then turn off the heat. *Keep the lid on* and allow the fish to cool completely in the water (the fish should be just barely covered in the water).

To serve: When the fish is barely cold, remove from the fish kettle and drain for a few minutes. Line a large board or serving dish with fresh crisp lettuce leaves, top with sprigs of watercress, lemon balm and fennel and fennel flowers if available. Carefully slide the salmon onto the board. Just before serving, peel off the top skin, leave the tail and head intact. (We don't scrape off the brown flesh in the centre because it tastes good.) Pipe a line of home-made Mayonnaise along the centre of the salmon lengthways, garnish with tiny sprigs of fennel and fennel flowers or very thin twists of cucumber. Put some segments of lemons around the dish between the lettuces and herbs. Resist the temptation to use any tomato or — horror of horrors — to put a slice of stuffed olive over the eye! The pale pink of the salmon flesh with the crisp lettuces and fresh herbs seems just perfect. Serve with a bowl of good home-made Mayonnaise (see page 4).

Whole Salmon or Sea Trout cooked in Foil

1 salmon *or* sea trout, 3.4–4 kg/8–9 lbs approx. sea salt and freshly-ground pepper	110 g/4 ozs/1 stick butter approx. sprig of fennel

Garnish

segments of lemon and sprigs of parsley *or* fennel	a large sheet of good quality tin foil

Preheat the oven to 180°C/350°F/regulo 4.

Clean and gut the fish if necessary, dry carefully. Put the sheet of tin foil on a large baking sheet, preferably with edges. Place the salmon in the centre of the sheet of tin foil. Smear butter on both sides and put a few lumps in the centre. Season with salt and freshly-ground pepper and put a sprig of fennel in the centre if you have it. Be generous with the butter, it will mix with the juices to make a delicious sauce to spoon over your cooked fish. Bring the tin foil together loosely and seal the edges well.

Bake for 90 minutes approx. (allow 10 minutes per 450 g/1 lb). Open the package, be careful of the steam. Test by lifting the flesh off the backbone just at the thickest point where the flesh meets the head. The fish should lift off the bone easily and there should be no trace of blood; if there is, seal again and pop back in the oven for 5 or 10 minutes, but be careful not to overcook it.

Serve hot or cold. If you are serving it hot, spoon the juices over each helping, or use the butter and juice to make a Hollandaise-type sauce by whisking the hot melted butter and salmon juice gradually into 2 egg yolks, and add a little lemon juice to taste. If the fish is to be served cold, serve with some freshly-made salads and a bowl of home-made mayonnaise. Garnish with parsley and fennel.

Grey Sea Mullet Baked with Butter

Serves 4

Grey sea mullet is possibly the most under-estimated fish in our waters at present. Its flavour and texture are in my opinion every bit as good as sea bass but it costs a fraction of the price, so search for it in your fish shops before everyone discovers it and the price goes up. Remember how cheap monkfish used to be a few years ago! Grey sea mullet has large scales which must be removed. It is wonderful poached, fried or baked.

1 grey sea mullet 1.6–1.8 kg/$3\frac{1}{2}$–4 lbs approx.
55–110 g/2–4 ozs butter

salt and freshly-ground pepper
sprig of fennel

Preheat the oven to 180°C/350°F/regulo 4.

Scale the mullet, wash and gut if necessary. Dry the fish well.

Take a large sheet of good quality tin foil. Season the fish inside and out. Smear with lots of butter and put a few knobs into the centre with a sprig of fennel if available. Don't put lemon wedges or bay-leaf or anything else—it doesn't need it. Place the fish in the centre of the tin foil, draw up the edges and sides and seal well so that no butter or juices can escape while cooking.

Bake for 45 minutes approx. in a moderate oven. Test to see if the fish is cooked by lifting up some of the flesh off the bone near the head. There should be no trace of pink and it should lift off the bone easily. Put the whole package onto a serving dish. Garnish with a few sprigs of fennel and 4 lemon segments. Serve right away. Remove the skin as you serve and spoon the buttery cooking juices over the fish.

Monkfish with Cucumber and Tomato Hollandaise

Serves 4

**675 g/1½ lbs monkfish tail cut
into 1 cm/½ inch collops**

Poaching liquid
2.3 L/4 pints/10 cups water

**14 g/1 tablesp./4 American teasp.
salt**

Cucumber and Tomato Hollandaise
2 egg yolks
**125 g/4 ozs/1 stick butter cut into
dice**
1 dessertsp. cold water
1 teasp. lemon juice approx.
**⅓ of a cucumber, peeled and cut
into tiny dice**

7 g/¼ oz butter
**2 very ripe firm tomatoes to yield
2 tablesp. tomato concassé
approx.**
**salt, freshly-ground pepper and
sugar**
1 teasp. finely-chopped fennel

Garnish
sprigs of fresh fennel

First make the sauce. Put the egg yolks in a heavy stainless steel saucepan on a very low heat, or in a bowl over hot water. Add water and whisk thoroughly. Add the butter bit by bit, whisking all the time. As soon as one piece melts, add the next piece. The mixture will gradually thicken, but if it shows signs of becoming too thick or slightly 'scrambling', remove from the heat immediately and add a little cold water if necessary. Do not leave the pan or stop whisking until the sauce is made. Finally add the lemon juice to taste. If the sauce is slow to thicken it may be because you are excessively cautious and the heat is too low. Increase the heat slightly and continue to whisk until the sauce thickens to coating consistency. Pour into a bowl and keep warm.

Melt 7 g/¼ oz of butter and toss the tiny dice of cucumber in it for 1–2 minutes. Add to the Hollandaise Sauce.

Pour boiling water over the tomatoes, count to ten, pour off the water and peel. Cut in half and remove the seeds with a teaspoon or melon baller, cut the flesh into the same size dice as the cucumber. Sprinkle with salt, freshly-ground pepper and sugar and keep aside.

Just before serving, bring the 2.3 L/4 pints/10 cups of water to the boil and add 1 tablespoon of salt. Add the monkfish collops, bring back to the boil and *simmer* for 4–5 minutes or until the pieces are no longer opaque, but completely white and tender. Drain the monkfish thoroughly.

To serve: Put into a serving dish or arrange overlapping slices on individual plates. Drain the tomato concassé and add to the sauce with the finely-chopped fennel. Taste. Add a little hot water if the sauce is too thick. Spoon carefully over the fish. Garnish with sprigs of fennel and serve immediately.

Baked Plaice or Sole with Herb Butter*

Serves 4

This is a master recipe which can be used not only for plaice and sole but for all very fresh flat fish, e.g. brill, turbot, dabs, flounder and lemon sole. Depending on the size of the fish, it may be served as a starter or a main course. It may be served not only with Herb Butter but with any other complementary sauce, e.g. Hollandaise, Mousse-line, Beurre Blanc, Lobster or Champagne.

4 very fresh plaice *or* sole on the bone	**4 teasp. mixed finely-chopped fresh parsley, chives, fennel and thyme leaves**
55–110 g/2–4 ozs/4–8 tablesp. butter	**salt and freshly-ground pepper**

Preheat the oven to 190°C/375°F/regulo 5.

Turn the fish on its side and remove the head. Wash the fish and clean the slit very thoroughly. With a sharp knife, cut through the skin right round the fish, just where the 'fringe' meets the flesh. Be careful to cut neatly and to cross the side cuts at the tail or it will be difficult to remove the skin later on.

Sprinkle the fish with salt and freshly-ground pepper and lay them in 7 mm/$\frac{1}{4}$ inch of water in a shallow baking tin. Bake in a moderately hot oven for 20–30 minutes according to the size of the fish. The water should have just evaporated as the fish is cooked. Check to see whether the fish is cooked by lifting the flesh from the bone at the head; it should lift off the bone easily and be quite white with no trace of pink.

Meanwhile, melt the butter and stir in the freshly-chopped herbs. Just before serving catch the skin down near the tail and pull it off gently (the skin will tear badly if not properly cut. Lift the fish onto hot plates and spoon the herb butter over them. Serve immediately.

24

Baked Turbot or Brill with Sauce Mousseline

Serves 4

**1 turbot *or* brill, 1.8 kg/4 lbs
  approx. in weight**

Sauce Mousseline
**2 egg yolks
110 g/4 ozs/½ cup unsalted butter
2 teasp. lemon juice
4 fl ozs/½ cup whipped cream**

**1 heaped teasp./1 American
  teasp. very finely-chopped
  chives**

Preheat the oven to 190°C/375°F/regulo 5.

Turn the fish on its side and remove the head. Wash the fish and clean the slit very thoroughly. With a sharp knife, cut through the skin right round the fish, just where the 'fringe' meets the flesh. Be careful to cut neatly and to join the side cuts at the tail or it will be difficult to remove the skin later on.

Sprinkle the fish with salt and freshly-ground pepper and lay it in 7 mm/¼ inch of water in a shallow baking tin. Bake in a moderately hot oven for 40–45 minutes, according to the size of the fish. The water should have just evaporated as the fish is cooked. Check to see whether the fish is cooked by lifting the flesh from the bone at the head; it should lift off the bone easily and be quite white with no trace of pink.

Meanwhile, make the Sauce Mousseline. Put the egg yolks in a heavy stainless steel saucepan on a low heat, or in a bowl over hot water. Add water and whisk thoroughly. Add butter bit by bit, whisking all the time. As soon as one piece melts, add the next piece; it will gradually thicken. If it shows signs of becoming too thick or slightly 'scrambling', remove from the heat immediately and add a little cold water if necessary. Do not leave the pan or stop whisking until the sauce is made. Add the lemon juice to taste. Keep the sauce warm until the fish is ready to serve.

When the fish is cooked, get 4 hot plates. Peel the dark skin from the top of the fish and carefully lift the top 2 fillets onto 2 plates. Turn the fish over, lift off the white skin underneath and place these 2 fillets onto the other 2 plates.

Fold the softly-whipped cream and finely-chopped chives into the sauce. Spoon over the fish fillets and serve immediately.

Cod Baked with Cream and Bay-leaves, with Duchesse Potato*

Serves 6

This master recipe can be used for most round fish, e.g. haddock, pollock, grey sea mullet, ling, hake etc. Salmon and sea trout are delicious in this way or with a mixture of fresh herbs, e.g. parsley, fennel, lemon balm and chives.

6 portions of cod (allow 170 g/6 ozs approx. filleted fish per person)
1 tablesp. finely-chopped onion
salt and freshly-ground pepper

30 g/1 oz/$\frac{1}{4}$ stick butter
3–4 fresh bay-leaves
light cream to cover the fish, approx. 300 ml/$\frac{1}{2}$ pint/10 fl ozs
roux (see page xi)

Enrichment
15 g/$\frac{1}{2}$ oz butter *or* 1–2 tablesp. Hollandaise Sauce (optional, see page 18)

Melt the butter in a pan. Fry the onion gently for a few minutes until soft but not coloured. Put the cod in the pan and cook on both sides for 1 minute. Season with salt and freshly-ground pepper. Add bay-leaves. Cover with cream or creamy milk and simmer with the lid on for 5–10 minutes, until the fish is cooked. Remove the fish to a serving dish. Bring the cooking liquid to the boil and lightly thicken with roux. Whisk in the remaining butter or Hollandaise as an enrichment, check the seasoning. Coat the fish with sauce and serve immediately.

This dish can be prepared ahead and reheated and it also freezes well. Reheat in a moderate oven 180°C/350°F/regulo 4, for anything from 10–30 minutes, depending on the size of the container.

For a delicious starter, put the Cod with Cream and Bay-leaves into scallop shells which have been piped around the edge with a little ruff of Duchesse Potato (see below). For a dinner party the Duchesse Potato can be piped around a large serving dish with the cod in the centre. Garnish with bay-leaves before serving.

Duchesse Potato

Serves 4

900 g/2 lbs unpeeled potatoes,
  preferably Golden Wonders *or*
  Kerrs Pinks
300 ml/$\frac{1}{2}$ pint/10 fl ozs creamy
  milk

1–2 egg yolks *or* 1 whole egg and
  1 egg yolk
30–55 g/1–2 ozs/$\frac{1}{4}$ –$\frac{1}{2}$ stick butter

Scrub the potatoes well. Put them into a saucepan of cold water, add a good pinch of salt and bring to the boil. When the potatoes are about half cooked, 15 minutes approx. for 'old potatoes', strain off two-thirds of the water, replace the lid on the saucepan, put onto a gentle heat and allow the potatoes to steam until they are cooked.

Peel immediately by just pulling off the skins, so you have as little waste as possible; mash while hot (see below). (If you have a large quantity, put the potatoes into the bowl of a food mixer and beat with the spade.)

While the potatoes are being peeled, bring about 300 ml/$\frac{1}{2}$ pint of milk to the boil. Beat the eggs into the hot mashed potatoes, and add enough boiling creamy milk to mix to a soft light consistency suitable for piping; then beat in the butter, the amount depending on how rich you like your potatoes. Taste and season with salt and freshly-ground pepper.

Note: If the potatoes are not peeled and mashed while hot and if the boiling milk is not added immediately, the Duchesse Potato will be lumpy and gluey.

If you only have egg whites they will be fine and will make a delicious light mashed potato also.

Sea Trout with Cream and Fresh Herbs

Serves 2

450 g/1 lb sea trout fillets
2 teasp./2 American teasp.
  chopped onion
15 g/$\frac{1}{2}$ oz/1 tablesp. butter
240 ml/8 fl ozs/1 cup creamy milk
  (we use $\frac{1}{2}$ cream and $\frac{1}{2}$ milk)

30 g/1 oz/2 tablesp./$\frac{1}{2}$ cup
  chopped herbs: fennel, chives,
  parsley, chervil and thyme
  leaves
salt and freshly-ground pepper
roux (optional, see page xi)

Garnish
sprigs of fresh fennel

Choose a frying pan that is just big enough to hold the fish in a single layer. Melt the butter and fry the onion gently in it for 2 minutes. Add the trout and brown on both sides. Season with salt and freshly-ground pepper. Cover with creamy milk and 1 tablespoon of chopped herbs; bring it to simmering point. Cover the pan with a tight-fitting lid and cook on a gentle heat for 5–10 minutes approx. Keep a good eye on the fish as it's easy to overcook it. Just as soon as the fish is pale pink and no longer opaque, remove it to a serving dish. Bring the pan juices back to the boil, and thicken slightly by whisking in a little roux or by reducing the liquid. Add the remainder of the freshly-chopped herbs. Taste and correct seasoning if necessary. Spoon the sauce over the fish. Garnish it with sprigs of fresh fennel and serve immediately.

Poultry

Chicken used to be the greatest luxury about twenty years ago. My grandfather used to bring us chickens that he specially reared on his farm, but they were always for special occasions, and later at boarding school—delight of delights—we used to get chicken for lunch on Mother Prioress's feast day. The excitement, I remember it still! Perhaps it's just nostalgia but I'm quite sure that chicken tasted much more delicious then. Nowadays, chicken is less expensive and is arguably the most popular meat of all. The birds are intensively reared and produced on a large scale in not very humane conditions, so while the price has come down considerably, flavour has suffered correspondingly. As a result, there is inevitably a small but steadily growing demand for free-range chickens and eggs. These are more expensive to produce so the consumer must be prepared to pay a little extra for the naturally-reared bird with superior flavour.

When you are buying a chicken make sure to choose a good plump bird with unblemished skin. Just about every bit of a chicken can be used, so ask for the giblets also. The heart, neck and gizzard may be added to your stock pot and the chicken liver may form the basis of the delicious Ballymaloe Chicken Liver Pâté. The little lump of fat just inside the vent needn't be wasted either; if the chicken is free-range, this fat can be rendered down in a low oven and the resulting chicken fat is wonderful for roasting or sautéing potatoes. In a battery-reared chicken this fat can taste nasty, so just discard it.

Casserole roasting which is the method we use for Casserole Roast Chicken with Tarragon is a tremendously useful technique. It can be used not only to cook chicken, but also for turkey, pheasant and guinea-fowl. The herb we use here is French tarragon but you could use marjoram or thyme or a mixture of fresh herbs or even watercress. You can also cook the chicken on a bed of vegetables, for example in the recipe for Casserole Roast Chicken with Leeks and Bacon, or Pheasant with Port and Celery. Again, this technique can also be used for turkey, pheasant or guinea fowl, in fact it's particularly good for pheasant which can sometimes be dry. So you see there are many variations on this theme. The sauce is made from the skimmed juices in the bottom of the casserole, with or without the addition of cream.

Casserole Roast Chicken with Tarragon*

Serves 4–6

There are two kinds of tarragon, French and Russian, but we prefer to use French in this recipe because it has a rather better flavour than the Russian variety. Unfortunately French tarragon is more difficult to come by than Russian because it is propagated by root cuttings: you can't just grow it from seed like the Russian tarragon. French tarragon grows to a height of about 23 cm/9 inches, whereas the Russian will grow to about 1.25m/4 ft in the Summer.

1 x 1½ kg/3½ lbs chicken (free-range if possible)
1 tablesp. freshly-chopped French tarragon and 1 sprig of tarragon
30 g/1 oz/¼ stick butter
150 ml/¼ pint/5 fl ozs cream

salt and freshly-ground pepper
½–1 tablesp. freshly-chopped French tarragon (for sauce)
150 ml/¼ pint/5 fl ozs home-made chicken stock (optional)
roux (optional, see page xi)

Garnish
sprigs of fresh tarragon

Preheat the oven to 190°C/375°F/regulo 5.

Remove wing tips and wish bone and keep for stock. Season the cavity of the chicken with salt and freshly-ground pepper and stuff a sprig of tarragon inside. Chop the remaining tarragon and mix with two-thirds of the butter. Smear the remaining butter over the breast of the chicken, place breast-side down in a casserole and allow it to brown over a gentle heat. Turn the chicken breast-side up and smear the tarragon butter over the breast and legs. Season with salt and freshly-ground pepper. Cover the casserole and cook in a moderate oven for 1¼–1½ hours.

Test to see if the chicken is cooked, remove to a carving dish and allow to rest for 10–15 minutes before carving. (To test if the chicken is cooked, pierce the flesh between the breast and thigh. This is the last place to cook, so if there is no trace of pink here and if the juices are clear, the chicken is certainly cooked.) Spoon the surplus fat from the juices, blend in the cream and boil up the sauce to thicken it. Alternatively, just bring the liquid to the boil and whisk in a little roux (see page xi) until the sauce thickens slightly. Add a little freshly-chopped tarragon if necessary, taste and correct seasoning.

Carve the chicken into 4 or 6 helpings; each person should have a portion of white and brown meat. Arrange on a serving dish, nap with the sauce and serve.

Note: Some chickens yield less juice than others. If you need more sauce, add a little home-made chicken stock with the cream. If the sauce is thickened with roux this dish can be reheated.

Casserole Roast Chicken with Leeks and Bacon

Serves 4–6

1 x 1.56 kg/3½ lbs chicken
  (preferably free-range)
225 g/8 ozs streaky bacon
450 g/1 lb/2 cups leeks, trimmed
15 g/½ oz/⅛ stick of butter
1 splash of sunflower oil

146 ml/8 fl ozs/1 cup chicken
  stock *or* water
146 ml/8 fl ozs/1 cup light cream
salt and freshly-ground pepper
roux (optional, see page xi)

Garnish
15 g/½ oz/1 tablesp./¼ cup
  chopped parsley

Preheat the oven to 180°C/350°F/regulo 4.

Cut the white part of the leeks into rounds and wash them well. Cut the rind from the bacon and cut into 1 cm/½ inch cubes.

Remove the lumps of fat from inside the vent end of the chicken. Season with salt and freshly-ground pepper. Rub the butter over the breast and legs of the chicken and put it breast-side down into a casserole. Allow it to brown on a gentle heat; this can take 5 or 8 minutes. As soon as the breast is golden, remove from the casserole and keep aside. Add the pieces of bacon to the casserole with a splash of oil. Cook the bacon until the fat runs and the bacon is golden. Then add the sliced leeks and toss together in the bacon fat. Season with freshly-ground pepper, but no salt as the bacon will probably be salty enough. Then replace the chicken on top of the leeks and bacon. Cover the casserole and put into a moderate oven for 1¼ –1½ hours.

When the chicken is cooked, remove to a serving dish. Lift out the leeks and bacon with a perforated spoon and put into the centre of a hot serving dish.

Skim the juices of all fat, add the chicken stock and cream, and bring to the boil. Thicken by whisking in a little roux. The sauce should not be too thick, just thick enough to coat lightly the back of a spoon. Allow to simmer on a low heat while you carve the chicken.

Carve the chicken into 4 or 6 helpings, depending on how hungry you all are; everyone should get a portion of white and brown meat. Arrange the leeks and bacon around the chicken. Taste the sauce and add a little more salt and freshly-ground pepper if necessary. If the sauce has become too thick, add a little water. Spoon the hot sauce over the chicken, sprinkle with chopped parsley and serve.

Chicken with Rosemary and Tomatoes

Serves 4–6

1 x 1.6 kg/3$\frac{1}{2}$ lbs chicken (preferably free-range)
3 medium-sized potatoes
3 medium-sized onions
5–6 medium-sized very ripe tomatoes

30 g/1 oz/$\frac{1}{4}$ stick butter
1 tablesp. olive oil
sprig of rosemary *or* 1 teasp. thyme leaves
salt and freshly-ground pepper

Preheat the oven to 180°C/350°F/regulo 4.

If possible, remove the wishbone from the neck end of the chicken for ease of carving. Remove the lump of fat from inside the vent end of the chicken and put aside. Season the cavity with salt and freshly-ground pepper. Smear the breast with 15 g/$\frac{1}{2}$ oz of butter, put the chicken breast-side down into a casserole (preferably an oval one that will just fit the chicken) and allow to brown on a *gentle heat* for 5 or 6 minutes.

Meanwhile, peel and thickly slice the onions, potatoes and tomatoes. Chop the rosemary finely. Remove the chicken to a plate, add the remaining 15 g/$\frac{1}{2}$ oz butter and 1 tablespoon of olive oil to the casserole. Toss the potatoes, onions and tomatoes in the fat and oil. Sprinkle with chopped rosemary, salt and freshly-ground pepper. Cover and cook for 5–6 minutes. Put the chicken on top of the vegetables and cover. Cook in a moderate oven for 1$\frac{1}{4}$ hours approx.

Carve the chicken and serve surrounded with the potatoes, tomatoes and onions. De-grease the juices, bring to the boil and spoon over the chicken and vegetables. Serve sprinkled with chopped parsley.

Turkey Baked with Marjoram

Serves 12–14

1 x 4.5–5.4 kg/10–12 lbs turkey
110 g/4 ozs/1 stick butter
2 tablesp. finely-chopped marjoram and 2–3 sprigs of marjoram

900 ml/1$\frac{1}{2}$ pints/3$\frac{1}{2}$ cups light cream
salt and freshly-ground pepper
2 heaped tablesp. freshly-chopped marjoram

sprigs of marjoram

Preheat the oven to 180°C/350°F/regulo 4.

If possible remove the wish bone from the neck end of the turkey for ease of carving. Also remove the fat from the vent end, season the cavity with salt and freshly-ground pepper and stuff with 2 or 3 sprigs of fresh marjoram.

Smear the breast of the turkey with 55 g/2 ozs of soft butter. Put the turkey breast-side down into a large saucepan and cook on a gentle heat for 6–8 minutes, or until the skin on the breast turns golden. Turn the other way up and smear with 2 tablespoons of chopped marjoram mixed with another 55 g/2 ozs of butter. Season with salt and freshly-ground pepper. Cover with greaseproof paper and a tight-fitting lid. Cook in a moderate oven for 2–2½ hours. Test to see if the turkey is cooked: the juices should be clear and there should be no trace of pink between the thigh and the breast.

Remove the turkey to a carving dish, allow to rest while the sauce is being made. De-grease the cooking juices, add the light cream, bring to the boil, taste, and reduce if necessary to strengthen the flavour. Add 2 more tablespoons of freshly-chopped marjoram. Add the juices from the carving dish to the sauce. Taste, correct seasoning.

Carve the turkey and nap with the sauce. Garnish with sprigs of fresh marjoram.

Note: Use the turkey carcass to make stock on exactly the same principle as the chicken stock. Use for soups.

There are several varieties of marjoram; the one we use for this recipe is the annual sweet marjoram—origanum marjorana.

Pheasant with Apples and Calvados

Serves 4

Chicken or guinea fowl may also be used.

1 plump young pheasant	**salt and freshly-ground pepper**
15 g/½ oz/1 level tablesp. butter	**30 g/1 oz/¼ stick butter**
56 ml/2–2½ fl ozs/¼ cup Calvados	**2 dessert apples, e.g. Golden**
240 ml/8 fl ozs/1 cup cream	**Delicious**

Garnish
sprigs of watercress *or* chervil

Preheat the oven to 180°C/350°F/regulo 4.

Choose a casserole, preferably oval, just large enough to take the bird. Season the cavity, spread 15 g/½ oz of butter over the breast and legs of the pheasant and place breast-side down into the casserole. Allow it to brown on a gentle heat, turn over and sprinkle with salt and freshly-ground pepper. Cover with a tight-fitting lid and cook in a moderate oven for 40–45 minutes. Check to see that the pheasant is cooked (there should be no trace of pink between the leg and the breast). Transfer the pheasant to a serving dish and keep warm.

Carefully strain and de-grease the juices in the casserole. Bring to the boil, add the Calvados and ignite with a match. Shake the pan and when the flames have subsided, add the cream. Reduce until the sauce thickens, stirring occasionally; taste for seasoning. Meanwhile, carve the pheasant and arrange on a hot serving dish. Mask with the sauce.

Fry the peeled and diced apple in butter until golden. Put the apple in the centre and garnish the dish with watercress or chervil.

Pheasant with Celery and Port

Serves 4

Chicken or guinea fowl may also be used.

1 plump pheasant
45 g/1½ ozs/3 level tablesp. butter
1 finely-chopped onion
110 g/4 ozs streaky bacon
84 ml/4 fl ozs/½ cup port
290 ml/½ pint/1¼ cups chicken *or* pheasant giblet stock

salt and freshly-ground pepper
1 head of celery
185 ml/6 fl ozs/¾ cup cream
squeeze of lemon juice if necessary
roux (optional, see page xi)

Garnish
chopped parsley

Preheat the oven to 180°C/350°F/regulo 4.

Cut the rind off the bacon and cut into 5 mm/¼ inch cubes. Melt the butter in a casserole, add the bacon and onion and cook for a few minutes. Remove to a plate.

Smear a little butter on the breast of the pheasant and brown it in the casserole over a gentle heat. Return the onion and bacon to the casserole, then add port and stock. Bring to the boil, cover and cook in a moderate oven for 30 minutes.

Meanwhile, slice the celery into 10 mm/½ inch pieces, at an angle. Add to the casserole, packing it all around the pheasant. Season with salt and freshly-ground pepper and replace the lid. Cook for a further 30–35 minutes. Remove the pheasant as soon as it is cooked, strain and de-grease the cooking liquid. Arrange the celery and bacon in a serving dish, carve the pheasant into 4 portions and arrange on top of the celery.

Bring the cooking liquid back to the boil, add cream and simmer for 4 or 5 minutes to intensify the flavour. Thicken with a little roux if necessary. Taste for seasoning and sharpen with a little lemon juice. Spoon the sauce over the pheasant and celery, and serve scattered with chopped parsley.

Chicken Stock*

Home-made Chicken Stock is a wonderfully useful thing to have in your fridge or freezer. *Fond* is the name for stock in French; *fond* means foundation, which just sums up stock: stocks are the foundation of so many things — soups, sauces, casseroles etc. Making stock is really just an attitude of mind! Instead of absent-mindedly flinging things into the bin, keep your carcasses, giblets and vegetable trimmings and use them for your stock pot.

2–3 raw *or* cooked chicken carcasses *or* a mixture of both *or* 1 x 1.8 kg/4 lbs boiling fowl, disjointed	1 sliced onion
	1 leek, split in two
	1 stick of celery *or* 1 lovage leaf
	1 sliced carrot
giblets from the chicken, i.e. neck, heart, gizzard	few parsley stalks
	sprig of thyme
3.4 L/6 pints/120 fl ozs cold water approx.	6 peppercorns

Break up the carcasses as much as possible. Put all the ingredients in a saucepan and cover with cold water. Bring to the boil and skim the fat off the top with a tablespoon. Simmer for 3–5 hours. Strain and remove any remaining fat. If you need a stronger flavour, boil down the liquid in an open pan to reduce by one-third or one-half the volume. Do not add salt.

Note: Stock will keep several days in the refrigerator. If you want to keep it for longer, boil it up again for 5–6 minutes every couple of days; allow it to get cold and refrigerate again. Stock also freezes perfectly. For cheap containers use large yogurt cartons or plastic milk bottles, then you can cut them off the frozen stock without a conscience if you need to defrost it in a hurry!

In restaurants the stock is usually allowed to simmer uncovered so it will be as clear as possible but I usually advise people making stock at home to cover the pot, otherwise the whole house will smell of stock and that may put you off making it on a regular basis.

The above recipe is just a guideline. If you have just one carcass and can't be bothered to make a small quantity of stock, why not freeze the carcass and save it up until you have 6 or 7 carcasses plus giblets, then you can make a really good sized pot of stock and get best value for your fuel.

Chicken liver shouldn't go into the stock pot because it will cause a bitterness in the stock, but the livers make a wonderful smooth pâté which can be served in lots of different ways.

There are some vegetables which should not be put in the stock, e.g. potatoes because they soak up flavour and make the stock cloudy; parsnips — they are too strong; beetroot — they are too strong and the dye would produce a red stock! Cabbage or other brassicas give an off-taste on long cooking. A little white turnip is sometimes an asset, but it is very easy to overdo it. I also ban bay-leaf in my Chicken Stocks because I find that the flavour of bay can predominate easily and add a sameness to soups made from the stock later on.

Salt is another ingredient that you will find in most stock recipes, but not in mine. The reason I don't put it in is because if I want to reduce the stock later to make a sauce, it very soon becomes oversalted.

Ballymaloe Chicken Liver Pâté with Melba Toast*

Serves 10–12, depending on how it is served

This has been our pâté maison at Ballymaloe since the opening of the restaurant. We serve it in several different ways.
1. In little ramekins accompanied by hot crusty white bread.
2. In tiny pottery pots as part of a second course called 'Little pots of Pâté'.
3. We fill the Pâté into a loaf tin lined with cling film and, when it is set, slices are arranged on individual plates with a little dice of well-seasoned tomato concassé and then it is garnished with chervil or lemon balm.
4. For a buffet, the loaf-shaped Pâté is covered with a thin layer of soft butter, which is decorated with tiny rosettes of butter and thyme

flowers. The whole Pâté is then arranged on a bed of lettuces and garnished with herbs in flower.

5. Rosettes of Pâté can be piped onto tiny triangles of Melba Toast, tiny Ballymaloe Cheese Biscuits (page 75) or slices of cucumber. These rosettes must be served within an hour of being prepared and are very pretty. Garnish with a spot of tomato concassé and a little chervil.

6. Pâté can be formed into a roll, wrapped in cling film or greaseproof paper and refrigerated. Later the paper is removed and the roll of Pâté is decorated with rosettes of butter and thyme leaves and flowers.

225 g/8 ozs fresh chicken livers	1 teasp. fresh thyme leaves
30 ml/2 tablesp./$\frac{1}{8}$ cup brandy	1 large clove of garlic
200–300 g/8–12 ozs/1–2 cups butter (depending on how strong the chicken livers are)	salt and freshly-ground pepper clarified butter to seal the top

Wash the livers and remove any membrane or green tinged bits. Melt a little butter in a frying pan; when the butter foams add in the livers and cook over a gentle heat. Be careful not to overcook them or the outsides will get crusty; all trace of pink should be gone. Put the livers through a sieve or into a food processor. De-glaze the pan with brandy, allow to flame, add garlic and then scrape off with a spatula and add to the livers. Purée for a few seconds. Allow to cool, then add 225 g/8 ozs/1 cup butter and fresh thyme leaves. Season carefully, taste and add more butter if necessary. This Pâté should taste fairly mild and be quite smooth in texture.

Clarify some butter (see below) and run a little over the top of the Pâté which can then be put into little pots or into one large terrine. Serve with Melba Toast or hot white bread. This Pâté will keep for 4 or 5 days in a refrigerator.

Note: It is essential to cover Chicken Liver Pâté with a layer of clarified, or even just melted butter, otherwise the Pâté will oxidise and become bitter in taste and grey in colour.

Clarified Butter

Melt 225 g/8 ozs/1 cup butter gently in a saucepan or in the oven. Allow it to stand for a few minutes, then spoon the crusty white layer of salt particles off the top of the melted butter. Underneath this crust there is clear liquid butter which is called clarified butter. The milky liquid at the bottom can be discarded or used in a white sauce.

Clarified butter is excellent for cooking because it can withstand a higher temperature when the salt and milk particles are removed. It will keep covered in a refrigerator for several weeks.

Melba Toast

Serves 4

**2 thin slices of white bread
(sliced pan will do as long as
it's not too thick)**

Toast the bread on both sides. Cut the crusts off immediately and then split the slice in half. Scrape off any soft crumb, cut into triangles and put back under the grill, untoasted side up, for a few seconds until the edges curl up.

Serve with pâtés.

Beef and Lamb

Beef

Ireland with its lush green pastures has one of the very best climates anywhere in the world for the production of superb quality beef and as a nation we are very fond of beef. Make sure you choose a butcher who buys his meat not only for tenderness, but also for flavour. Fillet of beef is really never tough, but it can indeed be virtually tasteless. What you are looking for is a piece of *fresh* fillet of beef with a really 'beefy' flavour. It seems to me that the best-flavoured beef comes from well-reared Aberdeen Angus and Shorthorn. I personally very much regret the growing popularity of the continental breeds, e.g. Limousin and Charollais, which produce leaner meat with less flavour. That, we are told by the powers that be, is what the consumer wants: well it's certainly not what I want and I strongly question that it's what anyone else wants either! We have been brain-washed into believing that meat with any little bit of fat will kill us 'stone dead'. I doubt that too, but one thing I do know for certain is that meat must have a little bit of fat if it is to have a really good flavour. Cook the meat with the fat on, then leave it to the side of your plate if you don't want to eat it, but your lean meat will at least taste wonderful.

The recipe for Fillet of Beef with Mushrooms and Thyme Leaves is a recipe for a special occasion and makes the most of a nice piece of fillet of beef. The Fillet of Beef with Black, White and Pink Peppercorns is also delicious and takes even less time to make. I also wanted to include the great old favourite Boeuf Bourguignonne, because nothing can surpass this classic French beef stew when it's made with really good stewing beef and a bottle of wine! Everyone loves it and it's really warming fare for a Winter day. Carpaccio on the other hand, which is the famous Italian raw beef recipe, may not instantly appeal to you, but try it and you will be surprised at how appetising it is; 450 g/1 lb of beef can feed about 14–16 people served this way.

It's a great shame that so many people seem to have decided that they just don't like any kind of offal—they don't know what they are missing. I've converted several determined offal-haters by twisting their arms to taste a bit of calves' liver before they write off offal completely. Lightly cooked calves' liver is a revelation, it just melts in your mouth. It also has the advantage of cooking very quickly, in fact it is vital not to overcook it, otherwise it can, like any liver, become tough and leathery. In this recipe we add a little Irish Whiskey to the sauce to make it extra special and it's one of the great favourites on the menu at Ballymaloe. Young lamb's liver can be used instead if you cannot find calves' liver.

Fillet of Beef with Mushrooms and Thyme Leaves*

Serves 6

Fillet of Beef is always a treat nowadays and this delicious recipe for a special occasion makes a little beef go as far as possible.

1.010–1.125 kg/2$\frac{1}{4}$ – 2$\frac{1}{2}$ lbs fillet steak (allow 170–200 g/6–8 ozs sirloin *or* fillet steak per person)
15 g/$\frac{1}{2}$ oz/1 level tablesp. butter
1 dessertsp. olive oil
225 g/$\frac{1}{2}$ lb/4 cups sliced button mushrooms

30 g/1 oz/$\frac{1}{8}$ cup butter
3 tablesp./4 American tablesp. chopped shallot *or* spring onion
salt and freshly-ground pepper

For Sauce
150 ml/2$\frac{1}{2}$ fl ozs/$\frac{1}{4}$ pint red wine *or* dry Vermouth
150 ml/2$\frac{1}{2}$ fl ozs/$\frac{1}{4}$ pint home-made brown beef stock (see page 46)

290 ml/10 fl ozs/$\frac{1}{2}$ pint cream
roux (optional, see page xi)
$\frac{1}{2}$ teasp. fresh thyme leaves
a few drops of lemon juice

Garnish
tomato concassé
salt, freshly-ground pepper and sugar

flat parsley *or* watercress *or* chervil

The Sauce: Melt the butter in a frying pan and sweat the finely-chopped shallot on a gentle heat until soft but not coloured; remove from the pan. Increase the heat and sauté the mushrooms in small batches; season each batch and add to the onions as soon as they are cooked. Add the wine or Vermouth and stock to the pan and boil rapidly until the liquid has reduced to 75 g/$\frac{1}{8}$ pint approx. Add the cream and allow to simmer for a few minutes to thicken (whisk in a tiny bit of roux if you like), add the mushroom and onion mixture and the thyme leaves. Simmer for 1 or 2 minutes; don't allow the sauce to thicken too much or it will be heavy and cloying. Correct seasoning if necessary. If the sauce tastes too rich, add a squeeze of lemon juice. This is the sauce and it can be prepared several hours in advance and reheated later.

To prepare the beef: Trim the beef of any fat or membrane, cut into 55 g/2 ozs pieces.

To cook the beef: Melt a very little butter and some olive oil in a hot pan and when the foam subsides sauté the beef. Remember not to overcrowd the pan; the pieces of beef will only take 1–3 minutes on each side, depending on how you like it cooked. As soon as the beef is cooked, place the pieces on an upturned plate which rests on a larger plate to catch any juices.

To serve: Reheat the sauce, place the pieces of beef on individual plates or on a large serving plate and coat with the mushroom sauce. Garnish with tomato concassé and flat parsley or chervil.

Fillet of Beef with Black, White and Pink Peppercorns

Serves 4

The pink peppercorn is a reasonably new arrival in our speciality shops. Also called poivre rose and baie rose, it is a soft bright pink peppercorn with a peppery but sweet flavour. It is sold dried and can be ground in a mill. In fact it's not a true pepper at all, but the berry of a plant related to poison ivy. Some people are allergic to it, so use with caution!

4 fillet steaks, 170–225 g/6–8 ozs each
14 g/1 tablesp./4 teasp. olive oil

28 g/2 tablesp./$\frac{1}{8}$ cup brandy
150 ml/8 tablesp./$\frac{1}{2}$ cup cream

Pepper
1 teasp. black peppercorns (mignonette)

1 teasp. green peppercorns (washed)
2 teasp. pink peppercorns

Heat a heavy pan until very hot, add oil and sauté the steaks to the required degree: 3 minutes approx. each side for medium rare, 5 minutes approx. each side for well done. Remove the steaks and leave to relax on a warm plate while you make your sauce.

De-glaze the pan with brandy, then flame or reduce. Add green and black peppercorns. Crush the green peppercorns slightly with a wooden spoon in the pan. Add the cream and reduce for a few minutes, then add the juices from the steak. Season with salt and add the pink peppercorns; taste. Return the steaks to the pan and turn them in the sauce, then transfer to a warm plate and nap with the sauce. Serve at once.

Note: If you would like a little more sauce, add 3–4 tablespoons of home-made Beef Stock (see page 46) to the pan with the brandy and continue as above.

Mignonette of peppers means that the peppercorns should be roughly crushed, preferably in a pestle and mortar, but use whatever means are at your disposal—even if it involves putting them into a plastic bag and banging them with the bottom of a saucepan! Pepper ground in a pepper mill is too fine for this recipe.

Carpaccio with Mustard and Horseradish Sauce

Serves 12

Carpaccio is the ultimate recipe to make a little beef go a very long way. This sophisticated dish was invented in Harry's Bar in Venice and named for Carpaccio, the great 15th-century Venetian painter.

450 g/1 lb fillet of beef (fresh not frozen)

Sauce
2 egg yolks	**150 ml/$\frac{1}{4}$ pint light olive oil** *or*
2 tablesp. Dijon mustard	**sunflower oil**
1 tablesp. sugar	**1 tablesp. grated fresh**
28 ml/2 tablesp./8 teasp. wine	**horseradish**
vinegar	**1 good teasp. chopped parsley**

Garnish
24 tiny spring onions	**watercress** *or* **flat parsley**

First make the sauce: Put the egg yolks into a bowl and add the mustard, sugar and wine vinegar and mix well. Whisk in the oil gradually as though you were making Mayonnaise. Finally, add the grated horseradish and chopped parsley. Taste and season if necessary.

Chill the meat. Slice the beef fillet with a very sharp knife, as thinly as possible. Place each slice on a piece of oiled cling film, cover with another piece of oiled cling film. Roll gently with a rolling pin until almost transparent and double in size. Peel the cling film off the top, invert the meat onto a chilled plate, and gently peel away the other layer of film.

To serve: Spoon a little sauce onto the side of each plate, garnish with tiny spring onions and some flat parsley or sprigs of watercress.

Carpaccio may be served as a starter or main course, depending on the size of the helping.

Sauté of Calves Liver with Whiskey and Tarragon*

Serves 2

225 g–340 g/8–12 ozs calves liver,
  cut into 1 cm/½ inch slices
seasoned flour
15 g/½ oz butter
3 tablesp. whiskey
100 ml/4 fl ozs concentrated
  home-made brown beef stock
  (see page 46)

1 small clove of garlic
2 teasp. chopped fresh tarragon
50 ml/3 tablesp./¼ cup cream
salt and freshly-ground pepper

Garnish
2 sprigs of fresh tarragon

Heat the butter in a heavy frying pan until it foams. Dip the slices of liver in seasoned flour and fry gently on both sides. While the liver is still pink in the centre remove the meat to a warm serving plate. Pour in the whiskey; if cooking on gas, tilt the pan towards the heat, allowing the flame to leap in to ignite the whiskey. Light with a match otherwise. When the flames have died down, add the stock, garlic and tarragon. Reduce until the sauce thickens slightly, add the cream and boil again until the sauce lightly coats the back of a spoon. Taste for seasoning and add a little freshly-ground pepper and salt if necessary. Spoon the sauce over the liver, garnish with a sprig of tarragon and serve *immediately*.

Boeuf Bourguignonne

Serves 6

In this country, stew is generally regarded as something you feed the family but not your honoured guests. Not so in France, where this recipe for the most famous of all beef stews, Boeuf Bourguignonne, might be served for a special Sunday lunch or dinner with friends. After all it is not cheap to make: you need best-quality well-hung stewing beef and almost a bottle of red wine. As the name suggests it used to be made with Burgundy, but with current Burgundy prices I think I might settle for a good Beaujolais or a full-bodied Côtes de Rhone wine!

170 g/6 ozs streaky bacon
14–28 ml/1–2 tablesp./4–8 teasp.
  olive oil
1.35 kg/3 lbs stewing beef cut
  into 5 cm/2 inch cubes
1 carrot, sliced
1 onion, sliced
750 ml/1¼ pints/3 cups red wine:
  a full-bodied young wine, e.g.
  a Burgundy, Beaujolais or
  Côtes de Rhone would be
  perfect
425 ml/¾ pint/2 cups home-made
  brown beef stock (see page 46)

1 tablesp. tomato paste
1 bay-leaf
1 sprig of thyme
a 5 cm/2 inch piece of dried
  orange peel
2–3 cloves of garlic
salt and freshly-ground pepper
roux (optional)
18–24 small onions, depending
  on size
450 g/1 lb fresh mushrooms, cut
  in quarters

Remove the rind from the bacon and cut into 1 cm/½ inch cubes. Blanch and refresh if salty. Dry well on kitchen paper. Heat 1–2 tablespoons of olive oil in a frying pan, sauté the bacon until crisp and golden, and transfer it to a casserole. Turn up the heat so that the oil and bacon fat is almost smoking. Dry off the meat. Sauté it, a few pieces at a time, until nicely browned on all sides, and add to the casserole with the bacon. Toss the sliced carrot and onion in the remaining fat and add these too. If there is any fat left on the pan at this stage pour it off, then de-glaze the pan with wine, scraping the little bits of sediment on the pan until they dissolve. Bring to the boil and pour over the beef.

The casserole may be prepared ahead to this point. Allow it to get cold, cover and refrigerate overnight, or at least for a few hours. The wine will have a tenderising effect on the meat, and the herbs and other ingredients will add extra flavour as the meat marinades.

Bring the casserole to the boil, add enough stock to cover the meat, add in the tomato paste, dried orange peel, thyme, bay-leaf and the whole cloves of garlic. Season with salt and freshly-ground pepper. Bring to the boil, cover and simmer very gently either on top of the stove or in a low oven, 160°C/325°F/regulo 3 for 2–3 hours, depending on the cut of meat used. The meat should not fall apart: it should be tender enough to eat without too much chewing.

Meanwhile cook the onions and mushrooms. Peel the button onions. This task is made easier if you drop them in boiling water for 1 minute and then run them under the cold tap. 'Top and tail' them and then slip off the skins. Simmer gently in a covered casserole with about 1 cm/½ inch of water or beef stock — they will take about 30–35 minutes depending on size. A knife should pierce them easily.

Toss the quartered mushrooms a few at a time in a little olive oil in a hot pan. Season with salt and freshly-ground pepper.

When the meat is tender, pour the contents of the casserole into a strainer placed over a saucepan. Discard the herbs, sliced carrot and onion and orange peel. Return the meat to the casserole with the onions and mushrooms. Remove the fat from the liquid. There should be about 570 ml/1 pint of sauce. Taste, bring back to the boil and simmer. If the sauce is too thin or too weak, reduce for a few minutes, otherwise thicken slightly by whisking in a little roux. Pour over the meat, mushrooms and onions, bring back to the boil, simmer for a few minutes until heated through, and correct seasoning if necessary.

Sprinkle with chopped parsley and serve.

Boeuf Bourguignonne may be made a few days ahead and, within reason, the flavour even improves with keeping.

Brown Beef Stock

Brown beef stock is used for beef and game stews and for sauces.

2.5–2.7 kg/5–6 lbs beef bones, preferably with some scraps of meat on, cut into small pieces	2 cloves
	4 unpeeled cloves of garlic
	1 teasp. tomato purée
2 large onions, quartered	4 L/8 pints/20 cups water
2 large carrots, quartered	large bouquet garni, including
2 stalks celery, cut in 2.5 cm/ $\frac{1}{2}$ inch pieces	parsley stalks, bay-leaf, sprigs of thyme and a sprig of
10 peppercorns	tarragon

Preheat the oven to 230°C/450°F/regulo 8.

Put the bones into a roasting tin and roast for 30 minutes or until the bones are well browned. Add the onions, carrots and celery and return to the oven until the vegetables are also browned. Transfer the bones and vegetables to the stock pot with a metal spoon. Add the bouquet garni, peppercorns, cloves, garlic and tomato purée. De-grease the roasting pan and de-glaze with some water, bring to the boil and pour over the bones and vegetables. Add the rest of the water and bring slowly to the boil. Skim the stock and simmer gently for 5–6 hours. Strain the stock, allow it to get cold, and skim off all the fat before use.

This stock will keep for 2–3 days in the refrigerator. If you want to keep it for longer, boil it for 10 minutes, and then chill again. It can also be frozen.

Lamb

Irish lamb particularly has a wonderful flavour because most is still reared naturally outdoors on grass and, in the case of my butcher, on old pastures full of herbs and wild flowers. I've discovered that the flavour of meat comes not only from the breed of animal and the way it is reared, but also from what the animal feeds on. All over the countryside there are still local butchers who choose their own meat and understand about flavour, so shop around, and when you find a really good butcher ask him to point out the various cuts of meat to you because it's absolutely vital that you 'know your meat'. Otherwise, human nature being what it is, you may just be taken advantage of. When you do get a particularly good piece of meat, don't forget to tell your butcher it was good and then he will know that you're really interested and you will get an even better piece the next time.

My own marvellous butcher has a great saying that, 'there's no such thing as bad meat to a good cook'. In other words if someone complains about tough meat, it usually means that they haven't cooked it properly or else they have cooked it when the meat was too fresh. Lamb should be hung for seven to ten days, beef for ten to fourteen days, depending on the cut and the weather.

For Lamb Roast with Rosemary and Garlic or Lamb Roast with Garden Herbs, you can use not only the leg but also loin, or indeed shoulder (except it's a little tricky to carve on the bone). The former is wonderful served with a home-made Red Currant Jelly. The technique for Lamb Roast with Garden Herbs is very similar. Myrtle Allen came up with this recipe when she had her restaurant in Paris; she called it Lamb Roast with Irish Garden Herbs, and the French absolutely loved it served pink and cut in quite thick slices.

In Ireland, perhaps because of our history, we don't have a great culinary tradition but we have some wonderful recipes of which we can be justly proud. One of those is Irish Stew. This is the version we serve at Ballymaloe. We don't claim that this is the only authentic version, because there are many variations on the theme. Feelings run high on this point! People seem to divide into two main camps: those who believe that real Irish Stew should include carrots, and those who feel that it should have only mutton, onions and potatoes. We add carrots because they enhance the flavour and I like to add a sprig of thyme too. Other people add some pearl barley and still others slice some of the potatoes into the bottom of the pot to thicken the juices. I don't do this because, while it does indeed thicken the juices, it is rather inclined to soak up the flavour too; instead, I cover the top of the stew with the potatoes so they can steam. They taste wonderful and are flavoured with the meat juices.

Irish Stew is a marvellous dish for a chilly day—what I call 'comfort food'. When I think of Irish Stew I feel all warm inside. I remember sitting by the fire eating stew from a deep plate and I'm transported back in time to my childhood. Such a pity that Irish Stew is so seldom seen on restaurant menus. It deserves to be served more, particularly in restaurants on the tourist routes, because visitors in Ireland ask over and over again where they can find an Irish Stew.

Spiced Lamb with Aubergines on the other hand is a completely different flavour. The smokey taste of the aubergines and the nutty taste of the cumin evoke images of the Middle East.

Lamb Roast with Rosemary and Garlic*

Serves 8–10

1 x 2.7 kg/6 lbs leg of lamb (a
2.7–3.2 kg/6–7 lbs leg of lamb
will have about 620 g/1 lb 6
ozs bone)

4–5 cloves of garlic
2 sprigs of rosemary

For gravy
300 ml/½ pint/1¼ cups stock
(preferably home-made lamb
stock)

roux (optional)

Red currant Jelly optional

Choose a good leg of lamb with a thin layer of fat. With the point of a sharp knife or skewer, make deep holes all over the lamb, about 2.5 cm/1 inch apart. It is a good idea not to do this on the underside of the joint, in case somebody insists on eating their lamb unflavoured. Divide the rosemary sprigs into tufts of three or four leaves together.

Peel the garlic cloves and cut them into little spikes about the same size as a matchstick broken into three. Stick a spike of garlic into each hole with a tuft of rosemary. Cover and refrigerate for up to 24 hours if you have time.

Heat the oven to 200°C/400°F/regulo 6. Sprinkle the joint with salt and freshly-ground pepper and put it into a roasting tin in the oven. Reduce the heat to 180°C/350°F/regulo 4 after 20 minutes. Cook 1 hour approx. more for rare lamb, 1½ hours if it is to be well done. Remove the joint to a serving dish and allow it to rest while you make the gravy.

Spoon the fat off the roasting tin. Pour stock into the cooking juices remaining in the tin. Boil for a few minutes, stirring and scraping the pan well, to dissolve the caramelised meat juices (I find a small whisk ideal for this). Thicken with a very little roux if you like. Taste and add salt and freshly-ground pepper if necessary. Strain and serve the gravy separately in a gravy boat.

Serve with Roast Potatoes.

Red Currant Jelly*

Makes 3 x 450 g/1 lb jars

Red currant jelly is a very delicious and versatile product to have in your larder because it has so many uses. It can be used like a jam on bread or scones, or served as an accompaniment to roast lamb, bacon or ham. It is also good with some rough pâtés and game, and is invaluable as a glaze for fruit tarts, e.g. the Almond Tart with Raspberries which we do in the programme on desserts.

This recipe is a particular favourite of mine, not only because it's fast to make and results in delicious intense-flavoured jelly, but because you can use the left-over pulp to make a fruit tart, so you get double value from your red currants.

Red currants are in season in August, but they are by no means as common as raspberries and strawberries, so if you can find them be sure to buy some and freeze a few pounds to use for jelly and sauces during the Winter. They freeze perfectly even with the strings on.

900 g/2 lbs/8 cups red currants　　　　**900 g/2 lbs/8 cups granulated sugar**

Remove the strings from the red currants either by hand or with a fork. Put the red currants and sugar into a wide stainless steel saucepan and stir continuously until they come to the boil. Boil for exactly 8 minutes, stirring only if they appear to be sticking to the bottom. Skim carefully.

Turn into a nylon sieve and allow to drip through; do not push the pulp through or the jelly will be cloudy. You can stir it gently once or twice just to free the bottom of the sieve of pulp.

Pour the jelly into sterilised pots immediately. Red currants are very high in pectin so the jelly will begin to set just as soon as it begins to cool.

Note: Unlike most other fruit jelly, no water is needed in this recipe.

Roast Potatoes*

Everybody loves roast potatoes, yet people ask me over and over again for the secret of golden crispy roast potatoes.
1. Well, first and foremost buy good quality 'old' potatoes, e.g. Golden Wonders, Kerrs Pinks, Pennella, or British Queens. New potatoes are not suitable for roasting.
2. Peel them just before roasting.

3. Do not leave them soaking in water or they will be soggy inside because of the water they absorb. This always applies, no matter how you cook potatoes. Unfortunately, many people have got into the habit of peeling and soaking potatoes even if they are just going to mash them.

4. Dry potatoes carefully, otherwise they will stick to the tin, and when you turn them over you will lose the crispy bit underneath.

5. If you have a fan oven it is necessary to blanch and refresh the potatoes first, then proceed as below.

6. Heat the olive oil or fat in the roasting pan and toss the potatoes to make sure they are well coated in the olive oil or fat.

7. Roast in a hot oven, basting occasionally, for 30–60 minutes depending on size.

8. For perfection, potatoes should be similar in size and shape.

Lamb Roast with Garden Herbs

An average weight leg of lamb 3.345–3.4 kg/7$\frac{1}{2}$ –8 lbs will serve 8–10 people. Allow 170 g/6 ozs approx. per person.

1 leg of lamb

Herb marinade
38 g/1$\frac{1}{4}$ ozs/1 cup chopped herbs: parsley, thyme, lemon balm, mint, tarragon, chives, rosemary and marjoram*

112–224 ml/4–8 fl ozs/$\frac{1}{2}$–1 cup olive oil
salt and freshly-ground pepper
3 large cloves of garlic

Gravy
570 ml/1 pint/2$\frac{1}{2}$ cups lamb *or* **chicken stock**
2 teasp. freshly-chopped herbs as above

a little roux (see page xi)
salt and freshly-ground pepper

Garnish
sprigs of fresh mint and parsley

* If you don't have access to this variety, use whatever fresh herbs you have, e.g. parsley, chives, thyme and mint.

First make the herb relish. Peel the garlic cloves and make them into a paste. Put them with the olive oil, salt and fresh herbs into a food processor and whizz them round for about 1 minute or until it becomes a soft green paste, otherwise just mix in a bowl.

If possible remove the aitch bone from the top of the leg of lamb so that it will be easier to carve later, then trim the end of the leg. Score the fat

51

lightly, rub in the herb mixture and leave to marinade for several hours if possible.

Preheat the oven to 180°C/350°F/regulo 4 and roast for 1¼ hours approx. for rare, 1½ hours for medium and 1¾ hours for well done. When the lamb is cooked to your taste, remove the joint to a carving dish. Rest the lamb for 10 minutes before carving.

De-grease the juices in the roasting tin, add stock, bring to the boil and thicken with a little roux if desired. Just before serving, whisk in some knobs of butter to enrich the gravy and add some freshly-chopped herbs.

Note: A 3.2 kg/7 lbs leg of lamb will have 570–850 g/1 lb 6–14 ozs of bone.

Mint Sauce

15 g/1 tablesp./¼ cup finely-chopped fresh mint
10 g/2 teasp./2 American teasp. sugar
56 ml/3–4 tablesp./¼ cup boiling water

15 ml/1 tablesp./4 American teasp. white wine vinegar *or* lemon juice

Put the sugar and freshly-chopped mint into a sauce boat. Add the boiling water and vinegar or lemon juice. Allow to infuse for 5–10 minutes before serving.

Ballymaloe Irish Stew*

Serves 4–6

1.35 kg/2½–3 lbs mutton *or* lamb chops (gigot *or* rack chops) not less than 2.5 cm/1 inch thick
5 medium *or* 12 baby carrots
5 medium *or* 12 baby onions
8 potatoes *or* more if you like

570 ml/1 pint/2½ cups stock (mutton stock if possible) *or* water
1 sprig of thyme
1 tablesp. roux (optional, see page xi)

Garnish
1 tablesp. freshly-chopped parsley

1 tablesp. freshly-chopped chives

Preheat the oven to 180°F/350°F/regulo 4.

A Leg of Lamb with Rosemary and Garlic, ready for the oven

Clockwise from right
Green Salad; Fillet of Beef with Mushrooms and Thyme Leaves; Sauté of Calves Liver with Whiskey and Tarragon

Ballymaloe Vanilla Ice-cream served in an Ice Bowl

Meringue Gâteau with Kiwi Fruit

Almond Tart with Raspberries

Cut the chops in half and trim off some of the excess fat. Set aside. Render down the fat on a gentle heat in a heavy pan (discard the rendered down pieces).

Peel the onions and scrape or thinly peel the carrots (if they are young you could leave some of the green stalk on the onion and carrot). Cut the carrots into large chunks, or if they are young leave them whole. If the onions are large, cut them small; if they are small they are best left whole.

Toss the meat in the hot fat on the pan until it is slightly brown. Transfer the meat into a casserole, then quickly toss the onions and carrots in the fat. Build the meat, carrots and onions up in layers in the casserole, carefully season each layer with freshly-ground pepper and salt. De-glaze the pan with mutton stock and pour into the casserole. Peel the potatoes and lay them on top of the casserole, so they will steam while the stew cooks. Season the potatoes. Add a sprig of thyme, bring to the boil on top of the stove, cover and transfer to a moderate oven or *allow to simmer* on top of the stove until the stew is cooked, 1–1½ hours approx., depending on whether the stew is being made with lamb or mutton.

When the stew is cooked, pour off the cooking liquid, de-grease and reheat in another saucepan. Slightly thicken it with a little roux if you like. Check seasoning, then add chopped parsley and chives and pour it back over the stew. Bring it back up to boiling point and serve from the pot or in a large pottery dish.

Spiced Lamb with Aubergines

Serves 6

900 g/2 lbs shoulder of lamb	salt and freshly-ground pepper
2 aubergines	225 g/½ lb very ripe tomatoes *or* 1
1 large onion	tin of tomatoes
28 ml/2 tablesp./8 teasp. olive oil	1 large clove of garlic
3 teasp. chopped mint	1 heaped teasp. crushed cumin
3 teasp. chopped marjoram	seed

Preheat the oven to 180°C/350°F/regulo 4.

Cut the meat into 2.5 cm/1 inch cubes. Cut the aubergines into cubes about the same size as the lamb. Sprinkle them with salt and put in a colander to drain with a plate on top of them to weigh them down.

Heat the olive oil in a pan and sweat the sliced onion. Add the meat and allow it to colour, sprinkle with mint and marjoram and season. Transfer the meat and onions to a casserole.

Wash off the aubergines and drain them in kitchen paper; toss them in olive oil in the pan, season with salt and freshly-ground pepper and cook for 10 minutes. Add to the meat and cover. Skin the tomatoes, chop them up and put them in the casserole with the meat mixture. Add crushed garlic. Heat the cumin for a few minutes either in a bowl in the oven or in a frying pan, crush in a mortar and add to the casserole. Cook on a gentle heat or in a moderate oven for $1\frac{1}{2}$ hours approx. Taste, correct the seasoning and de-grease the cooking liquid if necessary. Serve with rice.

The Essential Salad!

Green Salad may be served with virtually every lunch or dinner, either instead of or as well as vegetables. It also has the magical effect of making you feel less full if you have overdone it a little!

It is often difficult to get just a plain green salad in a restaurant. When you ask for a green salad you will quite possibly be given a mixed salad with peppers, tomatoes, cucumbers etc., and whereas there are many variations on a theme of green salad, basically it should be made up of different kinds of lettuces and salad things. The variety of lettuces one can buy in the shops has improved out of all knowing. Up to recently, the only lettuce that was widely available was the soft butterhead lettuce, but now Chinese leaves, iceberg and raddichio are becoming easier to find and lately we have been able to buy several varieties of the frizzy lettuces e.g. endive and the lovely frilly bronze-tinted lollo rosso.

However, the variety on offer is small in comparison with all the wonderful salad leaves that one can grow, given a little space. You might like to try some of the following: green or bronze oak leaf lettuce, cos, raddichio trevisano, rocket or aruguala, lamb's lettuce, salad burnet, mizuna, sorrel, edible chrysanthemum leaves and golden marjoram. Depending on what the salad is to be served with, one can also add some edible flowers for extra excitement and pzazz. Our favourites are tiny pansies or violas, borage flowers, nasturtium flowers and tiny leaves, chive or wild garlic blossoms, rocket flowers. So gather up whatever you can for your salad bowl, wash and dry them carefully and then make the dressing.

The dressing will depend on the quality of your oils and vinegars. Use a wine vinegar and olive oil or a mixture of olive and a lighter oil, e.g. sunflower or arachide oil. A basic French dressing is usually one part vinegar to three parts oil, salt, freshly-ground pepper and perhaps a spot of garlic and mustard. We make many different kinds of dressings, but Billy's French Dressing, named for a chef in the Ballymaloe kitchen called Billy Motherway, seems to be a great favourite. We usually liquidise the ingredients, but this is not necessary if you make a paste of the garlic and chop the herbs finely.

Any dressing is best on the day it's made, but if you would like to keep it, add the herbs and garlic just before you serve it. I find the garlic becomes a little bitter if the dressing is kept for a few days and the herbs lose their fresh green colour. Some people also like to add a pinch of sugar to the dressing: that's fine, though not at all 'French'. Be careful not to make it too sweet!

The greatest discovery I've made as far as salad is concerned in the last few years is the salad mix Mesculum, Saladisi or Mysticana, depending on what brand name you buy. (See end for names of seed merchants.)* Basically this is a mixture of seeds in a packet which you can scatter on to some peat moss in a seed tray, and leave on your window or greenhouse or garden. In a few weeks a great assortment of different lettuces and salad things both green and bronze will emerge and then you just cut with a knife, wash and dry and put into your salad bowl. You can leave it to recover for another few weeks and cut again once or, if you are lucky, twice more. We plant Mesculum in succession and find it tremendously useful.

* Seed stockists
Mackeys Seeds, Mary Street, Dublin 1
Garden World, 6 Camden Quay, Cork
Munster Seeds, Maylor Street, Cork
All stockists of Thompson-Morgan Seeds
Suffolk Herbs, Sawyers Farm, Little Conrad, Sudbury, Suffolk, England
Kilkenny Herbs, Imokilly Orchards, Shanagarry, Co. Cork deliver fresh herbs and edible flowers all round the country.

Green Salad with Billy's French Dressing*

50 ml/2 fl ozs/$\frac{1}{4}$ cup wine vinegar
150 ml/6 fl ozs/$\frac{3}{4}$ cup olive oil *or* a
  mixture of olive and other oils,
  e.g. sunflower and arachide
1 level teasp./$\frac{1}{2}$ American teasp.
  mustard (Dijon *or* English)
1 large clove of garlic

1 scallion *or* small spring onion
sprig of parsley
sprig of watercress
1 level teasp./$\frac{1}{2}$ American teasp.
  salt
few grinds of pepper

French Dressing

Put all the ingredients into a blender and run at medium speed for 1 minute approx., or mix oil and vinegar in a bowl, add mustard, salt, freshly-ground pepper and mashed garlic. Chop the parsley, spring onion and watercress finely and add in. Whisk before serving.

Green Salad

You will need a mild lettuce (e.g. the common butterhead) as the basis of the salad and as many of the following as you care to or can put in:

Finely-chopped parsley, mint or any herbs of your fancy; spring onions, dice of cucumber, mustard and cress, watercress, the white tips of cauliflower, tips of purple sprouting broccoli, iceberg lettuce, cos, raddichio, oakleaf, Chinese leaves, rocket, salad burnet, and any other interesting lettuces available.

Wash and dry the lettuces and other leaves very carefully. Tear into bite-sized pieces and put into a deep salad bowl. Cover with cling film and refrigerate, if not to be served immediately. Just before serving toss with a little French Dressing—just enough to make the leaves glisten. Serve immediately.

Note: Green Salad must not be dressed until just before serving, otherwise it will be tired and unappetising.

Green Salad with Edible Flowers

Prepare a selection of salad leaves (see above) and add some edible flowers, e.g. marigold petals, nasturtium flowers, borage flowers, chive flowers, rocket blossoms etc.; one or all of these or some other herb flowers could be added. Toss with a well-flavoured dressing just before serving.

This salad could be served as a basis for a starter salad or as an accompanying salad to a main course. Remember to use a little restraint with the flowers!

Puddings

It's such a joke, people spend so much time and energy talking in total seriousness about diets and healthy food, calories and all that non-sense. Then just watch the reaction when a sweet trolley comes round to the table in a restaurant! Caution is thrown to the wind as they cajole the 'trolley dolly' to pile their plates high with scrumptious 'puds'. The great Saturday night trick in Ballymaloe with a party of six or more is to start to eat your pud as fast as you can the minute it's served, so that by the time the last person at the table has got theirs you're ready to start all over again!

On the sweet trolley in Ballymaloe we always have a Meringue Gâteau and a Home-made Ice-cream among other things. The reason for this is that we use the egg yolks to make the delicious rich ice-creams and the egg whites to make the meringues. In that way there is no waste. At home if you decide to make ice-cream, make meringues also in the same session; you will then have two delicious puddings that will keep for ages, and don't forget to make an ice-bowl to serve the ice-cream in so you can dazzle the pals! It's also a great idea to make at least twice, or better still four times, the ice-cream recipe and the same of meringues, so you will have enough for several meals. Ice-cream of course freezes for months (don't forget to cover it even in the freezer or it will get what I call a 'fridgie' taste).

Meringues also keep for ages in an air-tight tin; if they do get a bit soft just pop them back into a low oven and then they will dry out and crisp again. They are one of the very best stand-bys—if you can manage to hide them away! The meringue recipe I use in the programme is virtually fool-proof and works even for people who are quite determined they can't make meringues! They are cooked at a higher temperature than usual so even if your oven is not accurate at very low temperatures and many aren't, it should be alright at 150°C/300°F/regulo 2. The meringue mixture can be baked in any shape or size you fancy and you could even produce a heart-shaped one for Valentine's Day or to bring on a proposal! I've included a recipe for Meringue with Kiwi Fruit and Meringue Nests to start you off.

My husband is a fruit grower, so I couldn't resist including some desserts made from fresh Summer fruit. The Summer Fruit Salad with Sweet Geranium Leaves, Summer Pudding and Blackcurrant Fool are three of his favourite recipes. His crowning glory is Summer Pudding, but he asks me to remind you not to forget to weight it down and to resist turning it out until the next day. He couldn't, and we had much merriment as a result!

The Almond Tart recipe is really a treasure—so quick and easy to make, it really is a prime example of what this whole series is about: 'Simply Delicious'.

Ballymaloe Vanilla Ice-cream Served in an Ice Bowl*

Serves 6–8

The Ballymaloe Ice-creams are very rich and very delicious, made on an egg mousse base with softly-whipped cream and flavouring added. Ice-creams made in this way have a smooth texture and do not need further whisking during the freezing period. They should not be served frozen hard. Remove from the freezer at least 10 minutes before serving.

30 g/1 oz/2 tablesp. sugar
120 ml/4 fl ozs/$\frac{1}{2}$ cup water
2 eggs yolks

$\frac{1}{2}$ teasp. pure vanilla essence
570 ml/1 pint/2$\frac{1}{2}$ cups *whipped cream*

Put the egg yolks into a bowl and whisk until light and fluffy (keep the whites for meringues). Combine the sugar and water in a small heavy-bottomed saucepan, stir over heat until the sugar is completely dissolved, then remove the spoon and boil the syrup until it reaches the 'thread' stage, 106°–113°C/223°–236°F. It will look thick and syrupy; when a metal spoon is dipped in, the last drops of syrup will form thin threads. Pour this boiling syrup in a steady stream onto the egg yolks, whisking all the time. Add vanilla essence and continue to whisk until it becomes a thick creamy white mousse. Softly whip the cream — it should just hold the print of the whisk. Measure and make sure you have 570 ml/1 pint of whipped cream. Fold the softly-whipped cream into the mousse, pour into a bowl, cover and freeze.

Ballymaloe Ice Bowl

This ice bowl was Myrtle Allen's brilliant solution to keeping the ice-cream cold during the evening on the sweet trolley in the restaurant. I quote from *The Ballymaloe Cookbook*.

'It took me twelve years to find the solution to keeping ice cream cold on the sweet trolley in my restaurant. At first we used to unmould and decorate our ices onto a plate. This was alright on a busy night when they got eaten before melting. On quieter occasions the waitresses performed relay races from the dining-room to the deep freeze. I dreamed about 19th century ice boxes filled from ice houses, to my husband's increasing scorn, and then I thought I had a solution. A young Irish glass blower produced beautiful hand-blown glass cylinders which I filled with ice-cream and fitted into beautiful tulip shaped glass bowls. These I filled with ice cubes. Six months later, however, due to either the stress of the ice or the stress of the waitresses, my bowls were gone and so was my money.

In desperation I produced an ice bowl. It turned out to be a stunning and practical presentation for a restaurant trolley or a party buffet.'

To make a Ballymaloe Ice Bowl: Take two bowls, one about double the capacity of the other. Half fill the big bowl with cold water. Float the second bowl inside the first. Weight it down with water or ice cubes until the rims are level. Place a square of fabric on top and secure it with a strong rubber band or string under the rim of the lower bowl, as one would tie on a jam pot cover. Adjust the small bowl to a central position. The cloth holds it in place. Put the bowls onto a Swiss roll tin and place in a deep freeze, if necessary re-adjusting the position of the small bowl as you put it in. After 24 hours or more take it out of the deep freeze.

Remove the cloth and leave for 15–20 minutes, by which time the small bowl should lift out easily. Then try to lift out the ice bowl. It should be starting to melt slightly from the outside bowl, in which case it will slip out easily. If it isn't, then just leave for 5 or 10 minutes more: don't attempt to run it under the hot or even the cold tap, or it may crack. If you are in a great rush, the best solution is to wring out a tea-towel in hot water and wrap that around the large bowl for a few minutes. Altogether, the best course of action is to perform this operation early in the day and then fill the ice bowl with scoops of ice-cream, so that all you have to do when it comes to serving the ice-cream it to pick up the ice bowl from the freezer and place it on the serving dish. Put a folded serviette underneath the ice bowl on the serving dish to catch any drips.

At Ballymaloe, Myrtle Allen surrounds the ice bowl with vine leaves in Summer, scarlet Virginia creeper leaves in Autumn and red-berried holly at Christmas. However, as you can see I'm a bit less restrained and I can't resist surrounding it with flowers! However you present it, ice-cream served in a bowl of ice like this usually draws gasps of admiration when you bring it to the table.

In the restaurant we make a new ice bowl every night, but at home when the dessert would be on the table for barely half an hour, it should be possible to use the ice bowl several times. As soon as you have finished serving, give the bowl a quick wash under the cold tap and get it back into the freezer again. This way you can often get 2 or 3 turns from a single ice bowl. One more point: don't leave a serving spoon resting against the side of the bowl or it will melt a notch in the rim.

Ballymaloe Coffee Ice-cream with Irish Coffee Sauce

Serves 6–8

2 tablesp./8 teasp. sugar
120 ml/4 fl ozs/$\frac{1}{2}$ cup water
2 egg yolks
$\frac{1}{2}$ teasp. vanilla essence

620 ml/1 pint/2$\frac{1}{2}$ cups whipped cream
3 teasp. instant coffee
$\frac{1}{2}$ teasp. boiling water

Irish Coffee Sauce
225 g/8 ozs/1 cup sugar
80 ml/3 fl ozs/$\frac{1}{3}$ cup water

240 ml/8 fl ozs/1 cup coffee
1 tablesp. Irish whiskey

Put the egg yolks into a bowl and whisk until light and fluffy. Put the sugar and water into a small heavy-bottomed saucepan on a low heat. Stir until all the sugar is dissolved and then remove the spoon and do not stir again until the syrup reaches the thread stage, 106°–113°C/223°–226°F. Continue to whisk until it fluffs up to a light mousse which will hold a figure of 8. Mix the instant coffee powder with just $\frac{1}{2}$ teaspoon of boiling water. Add some mousse to the paste and then fold the two mixtures together. Carefully fold in the softly-whipped cream. Pour into a stainless steel or plastic bowl, cover and freeze.

Irish Coffee Sauce

Put the sugar and water in a heavy-bottomed saucepan; stir until the sugar dissolves and the water comes to the boil. Remove the spoon and do not stir again until the syrup turns a pale golden caramel. Then add the coffee and put back on the heat to dissolve. Allow to cool and add the whiskey.

To serve: Scoop the ice-cream into a serving bowl or ice bowl. Serve the sauce separately.

Meringue Gâteau with Kiwi Fruit*

Serves 6–8

Lots of people are apprehensive about making meringues, but this, dare I say, is an almost 'fool-proof' recipe. Better still, it needs practically no skill to make, because you just add the icing sugar in with the egg whites at the beginning, so you don't have to worry about your 'folding in' technique. This meringue cooks faster and is baked at a higher temperature than ordinary Swiss meringue.

It is also tremendously versatile because it can be piped or spread into any shape you like: heart shapes, rectangles, squares, numbers e.g. 21, or letters, not to speak of various kinds of rosettes and twirls.

2 egg whites
11 g/4$\frac{1}{2}$ ozs/1 cup approx. icing
sugar

Filling
310 ml/$\frac{1}{2}$ pint/1$\frac{1}{4}$ cups whipped
cream
4–6 kiwi fruit peeled and sliced

Garnish
sprigs of fresh mint *or* **lemon**
balm

Cover a baking sheet with silicone paper (otherwise grease and flour the sheet very carefully). Draw out 2 × 19 cm/7$\frac{1}{2}$ inch circles on the paper or mark them with the tip of a knife on the flour.

Put the egg whites and all the icing sugar into a spotlessly clean bowl and whisk until the mixture forms stiff peaks; this can take 8–10 minutes in an electric mixer. You can whisk it by hand but it takes quite a long time, so if you have even a hand-held mixer it will speed up the operation. Divide the mixture between the 2 circles, spread evenly with a palette knife, making sure it's not too thin at the edges.

Bake in a low oven 150°C/300°F/regulo 2 for 45 minutes or until the meringues will lift easily off the paper. Turn off the oven and allow them to cool in the oven — with the door slightly ajar — for about 20–30 minutes. (If you take the meringues out of the hot oven and put them down on a cold work top they sometimes crack.)

To assemble: Put one of the meringue discs onto a serving plate. Pipe on the whipped cream (keep a little to decorate the top), cover with slices of kiwi fruit and put the second disc on top. Pipe 5 rosettes of cream onto the top, put a little piece of kiwi fruit on each and decorate with sprigs of fresh mint or lemon balm.

Note: Nuts are also delicious added to this recipe. *Fold* in 45 g/1$\frac{1}{2}$ ozs/ $\frac{1}{4}$ cup finely-chopped almonds just before you spread the meringue onto the silicone paper.

This Meringue Gâteau is also delicious filled with fresh strawberries, raspberries, loganberries, peaches or nectarines.

Silicone paper is sold under the brand name Bakewell and is available in many supermarkets and newsagents. It is invaluable for cooking meringue because it is non-stick so the meringue can be peeled off easily. The paper can be re-used several times.

Meringue Nests with Strawberries and Cream

Serves 6

2 egg whites

$4\frac{1}{2}$ ozs/1 cup approx. icing sugar

Filling
225g/8 ozs/1 cup strawberries

225 g/8 ozs/1 cup whipped cream

Garnish
fresh mint *or* lemon balm leaves

Cover a baking sheet with silicone paper (otherwise grease and flour the sheet very carefully). Draw out 4×9 cm/$3\frac{1}{2}$ inch circles on the paper or mark them with the tip of a knife on the flour.

Put the egg whites and all the icing sugar into a spotlessly clean bowl and whisk until the mixture forms stiff peaks. This can take 8–10 minutes in an electric mixer. Alternatively you can whisk it by hand but it takes quite a long time, so if you have even a hand-held mixer it will speed up matters a lot.

Put the meringue mixture into a piping bag with a number 5 rosette nozzle. Pipe a few blobs onto each circle and spread thinly with a palette knife. The meringue should not be more than $\frac{1}{2}$ cm/$\frac{1}{4}$ inch thick. Then carefully pipe a wall of meringue rosettes around the edge of each circle.

Bake in a low oven 150°C/300°F/regulo 2 for 45 minutes or until the meringue nests will lift easily off the paper. Turn off the oven and allow them to cool in the oven.

To assemble: Remove the stalks from the strawberries and cut them into slices lengthways. Pipe some whipped cream into each nest and arrange the slices of strawberries on top. Decorate with tiny rosettes of cream and garnish with fresh mint or lemon balm leaves.

Almond Tart or Tartlets with Raspberries*

Serves 12, makes 24 tartlets or 2×18 cm/7 inch tarts

110 g/4 ozs/1 stick butter
110 g/4 ozs/1 cup castor sugar

110 g/4 ozs/1 cup ground almonds

Filling
poached rhubarb *or* sliced fresh peaches *or* nectarines, fresh raspberries *or* loganberries, peeled and pipped grapes *or* kiwi fruit

290 ml/$\frac{1}{2}$ pint/$1\frac{1}{4}$ cups whipped cream

64

Garnish
lemon balm *or* **sweet geranium leaves**

Cream butter, sugar and ground almonds together. Put a teaspoon of the mixture into 24 shallow patty tins or 2 × 18 cm/7 inch sandwich tins. Bake at 180°C/350°F/regulo 4 for 20–30 minutes approx., or until golden brown. The tart or tartlets are too soft to turn out immediately, so cool in tins for about 5 minutes before removing from tins. Do not allow to set hard or the butter will solidify and they will stick to the tins. If this happens pop the tins back into the oven for a few minutes so the butter melts and then they will come out easily. Allow to cool on a wire rack.

Just before serving, arrange slices of peeled peaches or nectarines, whole raspberries, or peeled and pipped grapes on the base. Glaze with red currant jelly (red fruit) or apricot glaze (green or yellow fruit). Decorate with rosettes of whipped cream and garnish with lemon balm or sweet geranium leaves.

Note: Use shallow tartlet tins and best-quality ground almonds.

Red Currant Glaze

350 g/12 ozs red currant jelly   **1 tablesp. water approx.**

In a small stainless steel saucepan melt 350 g/12 ozs red currant jelly with 1 tablesp. water. Stir gently, but do not whisk or it will become cloudy. Cook it for just 1–2 minutes longer or the jelly will darken. Store any left-over glaze in an airtight jar and reheat gently to melt it before use. The quantities given above make a generous 300 ml/½ pint of glaze.

Apricot Glaze

350 g/12 ozs apricot jam   **2 tablesp. water**
juice of ¼ lemon

In a small stainless steel saucepan, melt 350 g/12 ozs apricot jam with the juice of ¼ lemon and 1–2 tablesp. water, enough to make a glaze that can be poured. Push the hot jam through a nylon sieve and store in a sterilised airtight jar. Reheat the glaze to melt it before using. The quantities given make a generous 300 ml/½ pint glaze.

Summer Fruit Salad with Sweet Geranium Leaves*

Serves 8–10

100 g/4 ozs/1 cup raspberries
100 g/4 ozs/1 cup loganberries
100 g/4 ozs/1 cup red currants
50 g/2 ozs/$\frac{1}{2}$ cup black currants
50 g/2 ozs/$\frac{1}{2}$ cup blackberries

50 g/2 ozs/$\frac{1}{2}$ cup blueberries (optional)
75 g/2$\frac{1}{2}$ ozs/$\frac{1}{2}$ cup fraises du bois (optional)

Syrup
400 g/14 ozs/2 cups sugar
16 fl ozs/$\frac{3}{4}$ pint/2 cups water

2 large *or* 6–8 medium-sized sweet geranium leaves

Put all the fruit into a white china or glass bowl. Put the sugar, cold water and sweet geranium leaves into a saucepan and bring slowly to the boil, stirring until the sugar dissolves. Boil for 2 minutes. Pour the *boiling* syrup over the fruit and allow to macerate for several hours. Remove geranium leaves. Serve chilled, accompanied by shortbread biscuits (page 76), softly-whipped cream or Ballymaloe Vanilla Ice-cream (page 60). Garnish with a few fresh sweet geranium leaves.

Note: The geranium we use in cookery and for garnishing is the lemon-scented Pelargonium Graveolens. It has pretty pale purple flowers in Summer.

Cultivated blueberries have been appearing in our shops from the end of July to the end of September for the last few years. They are quite delicious, so if you can find them, use them in this fruit salad.

Fraises du bois or Alpine strawberries are much more difficult to come by, unless you grow them in your garden; in this case you'll have lots, because after a few years they spread into every nook and cranny. They look so pretty, and the good varieties have a very intense flavour and a long fruiting season.

Summer Pudding

Serves 8

Everyone seems to become wistful when you mention Summer Pudding. Bursting with soft fruit and served with lots of softly whipped cream, it's one of the very best puddings of Summer. We actually make our Summer Pudding with cake but many people line the bowl with slices of white bread instead. I've used a mixture of fruit here, but it is also delicious made with black currants alone. Summer

Fruit Salad with Sweet Geranium Leaves also makes a successful filling, but you need to cook the black currants and red currants until they burst and then add the soft fruit. Remember to pour the fruit and syrup *boiling* into the sponge-lined bowl, otherwise the syrup won't soak through the sponge properly.

225 g/$\frac{1}{2}$ lb/2 cups black currants
225 g/$\frac{1}{2}$ lb/2 cups red currants
450 g/1 lb/4 cups raspberries *or*
225 g/$\frac{1}{2}$ lb/2 cups raspberries and
   225 g/$\frac{1}{2}$ lb/2 cups strawberries

580 g/21 ozs/3 cups granulated
   sugar
682 ml/24 fl ozs/3 cups water

For the sponge, see Great Grandmother's Sponge on page 73. Cut each sponge round in half, horizontally. Line a 1.7 L/3 pint bowl with the cake, crusty-side inwards. It doesn't matter if it looks quite patched, it will blend later.

Dissolve the sugar in the water and boil for 2 minutes, add the black currants and red currants and cook until the fruit bursts—about 3 or 4 minutes—then add the raspberries (and strawberries). Taste. Immediately, ladle some of the hot liquid and fruit into the sponge-lined bowl. When about half full, if you have scraps of cake put them in the centre. Then fill to the top with fruit. Cover with a layer of sponge. Put a plate on top and press down with a heavy weight. Allow to get cold. Store in the refrigerator for a minimum of 24 hours before serving, but it will keep for 4 or 5 days.

To serve: Unmould onto a deep serving dish and serve with any left-over fruit and syrup around it, and lots of softly-whipped cream.

Black Currant Fool

Serves 10–12

Fools can be made from many different kinds of fruit. We are particularly fond of black currant, gooseberry and rhubarb, but strawberry, raspberry, blackberry and fraughans (wild blueberries) are all wonderful too.

290 ml/$\frac{1}{2}$ pint/1$\frac{1}{4}$ cups water
225 g/$\frac{1}{2}$ lb/1 generous cup sugar

340 g/$\frac{3}{4}$ lb/3 cups black currants
softly-whipped cream

Dissolve the sugar in the water. String the black currants and cover them with syrup. Bring them to the boil and cook until soft, about 4–5 minutes. Liquidise or purée the fruit and press through a nylon sieve, measure. When the purée is quite cold, add up to an equal quantity of softly-whipped cream, according to taste.

Summer Fruit Salad with Sweet Geranium Leaves

Clockwise from right
Brown Soda Bread; Mummy's Sweet White Scones; Raspberry Jam; Ballymaloe Brown
Yeast Bread

Ballymaloe Brown Yeast Bread

Brown Soda Bread

Mummy's Sweet White Scones with Raspberry Jam and Cream

Breads and Jams

One of my very favourite things in the world is teaching people how to make bread. For some reason baking bread seems to provide such enormous satisfaction—it doesn't matter how long you've been doing it. I've been cooking most of my adult life, yet I still get a thrill every time I take a nice crusty loaf out of the oven. But I get even more satisfaction when I see the look of delight on my students' faces when they bake their first really good loaf. And it's a funny thing, but if you make a loaf of lovely fresh soda bread for a dinner party, it doesn't matter what other star turn you produce, everyone will remark on the bread—which may only have taken you five minutes to make.

I feel passionately that *everyone* should have good bread *every* day. I would just love *everyone* in the whole country to be able to bake delicious home-made bread: it's so quick and easy. Irish soda breads are particularly fast to make and I've shown you how to bake Brown and White Soda Bread and White Tea Scones, all of which are made by a similar method. None of them takes more than five minutes to mix.

We all know quite well that good wholesome fresh food is vital for our own health and that of our families, so let's start by making Brown Soda Bread, and when you've mastered that, let's move on to Yeast Bread. Many people have a hang-up about using yeast and the general feeling is that it's frightfully difficult and time-consuming. Fear not! Ballymaloe Yeast Bread is just the recipe for beginners. All you have to do is mix everything together. There's no kneading involved, and only one rising, and despite the fact that it's made from 100 per cent stone-ground wholemeal flour, it's light and has a wonderful rich and nutty flavour. Yeast differs from bread soda or baking powder in so far as it's a living organism, so you've got to be careful to treat it right. If you kill it, it won't rise your bread. Cold doesn't kill yeast but a temperature over 43°C/110°F does. Basically, yeast likes a lukewarm temperature and if possible something sweet to feed on. It feeds on sugar, and gives off bubbles of carbon dioxide and of course it's those bubbles which will rise your bread for you. I have easy access to fresh yeast and I prefer to work with it, but dried yeast makes a perfectly delicious loaf too (use half the quantity). You could use any sugar in this bread, e.g. brown sugar, golden syrup, honey or molasses, but it's treacle that gives Ballymaloe Brown Yeast Bread its particular flavour.

Whereas soda breads are best eaten on the day they are made,

Ballymaloe Brown Yeast Bread has the further advantage that it keeps perfectly for three or four days. Once they are mixed, soda breads should be put into a fully preheated oven right away, otherwise they will not rise properly. The same applies to risen yeast bread.

The dough for Ballymaloe Cheese Biscuits is quick to make but it must be rolled quite thinly and then pricked with a fork. They keep for ages in an air-tight tin and are good not only with cheese but with pâtés and are perfect for snacks. Great Grandmother's Cake is perfect of its type; both it and the Scones are irresistible filled with home-made raspberry jam and cream.

Many people feel that there is some great mystery to jam making: not so if you follow a few basic rules. For really good jam you *must* have really good fruit. The other great secret in my opinion is to make your jam in small quantities and to cook it for the minimum amount of time, then every pot will have perfect flavour and colour. If the fruit is as it should be, there is absolutely no need for artificial pectin or special sugar. A common belief is that if fruit is not good enough for anything else, it's alright for jam. Wrong! If the fruit is not perfect, cut your losses and dump it: don't throw good money after bad by making it into jam which will taste indifferent and soon go mouldy.

Nowadays many people have freezers, so the best thing is to buy your fruit in peak condition in season, when its flavour is best and the price is lowest; then freeze it immediately so you can make your jam in small quantities during the year, as you need it. Jam made from frozen fruit tastes much fresher and more delicious than jam kept on your storeroom shelf for five or six months.

Brown Soda Bread and Scones

Bicarbonate of soda (or bread soda) is the raising agent used in all soda breads. It is an alkali, and even though it is one of the ingredients used in baking powder, it can be used on its own to react with an acid, e.g. sour milk or buttermilk. This produces bubbles of carbonic acid which fill up with air and rise the bread. So the main thing to remember is: use bicarbonate of soda (bread soda) with buttermilk or sour milk, and baking powder—which is a mixture of acid and alkali substances— with ordinary milk.

675 g/1½ lbs/4½ cups brown wholemeal flour (preferably stone-ground)
450 g/1 lb/3¼ cups white flour
30 g/1 oz/¼ cup fine oatmeal
1 egg (optional)
30 g/1 oz/¼ stick butter (optional)

10 g/2 rounded teasp./2 American teasp. salt
10 g/2 rounded teasp./2 American teasp. bread soda, sieved
730–860 ml/1¼ –1½ pints approx./ 25–30 fl ozs sour milk *or* buttermilk

First preheat the oven to 230°C/450°F/regulo 8.

Mix the dry ingredients well together. Rub in the butter. Make a well in the centre and add the beaten egg, then immediately add most of the sour milk or buttermilk. Working from the centre, mix with your hand and add more milk if necessary. The dough should be soft but not sticky. Turn out onto a floured board and knead lightly, just enough to shape into a round. Flatten slightly to about 5 cm/2 inches approx. Put onto a baking sheet. Mark with a deep cross and bake in a hot oven 230°C/450°F/regulo 8 for 15–20 minutes, then reduce the heat to 200°C/400°F/regulo 6 for approx. 20–25 minutes, or until the bread is cooked and sounds hollow when tapped.

Brown Soda Scones

Make the dough as above. Form it into a round and flatten to 2½ cm/ 1 inch thick approx. Stamp out into scones with a cutter, or cut with a knife. Bake for about 30 minutes in a hot oven (see above).

Note: Bread should always be cooked in a fully pre-heated oven, but ovens vary enormously so it is necessary to adjust the temperature accordingly.

White Soda Bread and Scones*

450 g/1 lb/3¼ cups flour
1 level teasp./1 American teasp. sugar
1 level teasp./1 American teasp. salt

1 level teasp./1 American teasp. breadsoda, sieved
sour milk *or* buttermilk to mix—
350–425 ml/12–15 fl ozs/1½– 2 scant cups approx.

First fully preheat your oven to 230°C/450°F/regulo 8.

Sieve the dry ingredients. Make a well in the centre. Pour most of the milk in at once. Using one hand, mix in the flour from the sides of the bowl, adding more milk if necessary. The dough should be softish, not too wet and sticky. When it all comes together, turn it out onto a floured board, knead lightly for a few seconds, just enough to tidy it up. Pat the dough into a round about 4 cm/1½ inches deep and cut a deep cross on it to let the fairies out! Let the cuts go over the sides of the bread to make sure of this. Bake in a hot oven, 230°C/450°F/regulo 8 for 15 minutes, then turn down the oven to 200°C/400°F/regulo 6 for 30 minutes or until cooked. If you are in doubt, tap the bottom of the bread: if it is cooked it will sound hollow.

White Soda Scones

Make the dough as above but flatten the dough into a round 2.5 cm/1 inch deep approx. Cut into scones. Cook for 20 minutes approx. in a hot oven (see above).

Mummy's Sweet White Scones*

Makes 18–20 scones using a 7½ cm/3 inch cutter

900 g/2 lbs/6½ cups flour
170 g/6 ozs/1½ sticks butter
3 eggs
pinch of salt
60 g/2 ozs/⅓ cup castor sugar

3 heaped teasp./3 American teasp. baking powder
425 ml/15 fl ozs/scant 2 cups approx. milk to mix

For glaze
egg wash (see below)
granulated sugar for sprinkling on top of the scones

First pre-heat your oven to 250°C/475°F/regulo 9.

Sieve all the dry ingredients together. Rub in the butter. Make a well in the centre. Whisk the eggs with the milk, add to the dry ingredients and mix to a soft dough. Turn out onto a floured board. Knead lightly, just enough to shape into a round. Roll out to about $2\frac{1}{2}$ cm/1 inch thick and stamp into scones. Put onto a baking sheet. Brush with egg wash and sprinkle with granulated sugar.

Bake in a hot oven for 10–15 minutes until golden brown on top. Cool on a wire rack.

Serve split in half with home-made Raspberry Jam and a blob of whipped cream.

Egg wash: Whisk 1 egg with a pinch of salt. This is brushed over scones and pastry to help them to brown in the oven.

Fruit Scones

Add 110 g/4 ozs plump sultanas to the above mixture when the butter has been rubbed in. Continue as above.

Great Grandmother's Cake

170 g/6 ozs/1$\frac{1}{4}$ cups flour
170 g/6 ozs/$\frac{3}{4}$ cup castor sugar
3 eggs
125 g/4$\frac{1}{2}$ ozs/1 stick plus 1 level tablesp. butter

14 g/1 tablesp./1 American tablesp. milk
5 g/1 teasp./1 level American teasp. baking powder

Filling
225 g/8 ozs/$\frac{3}{4}$ cup home-made Raspberry Jam

285 g/10 fl ozs/1$\frac{1}{4}$ cups whipped cream

castor sugar to sprinkle

2 x 18 cm/7 inch sponge cake tins

Preheat the oven to 190°C/375°F/regulo 5.

Grease and flour 2 × 18 cm/7 inch tins and line the base of each with a round of greaseproof paper. Cream the butter and gradually add the castor sugar; beat until soft and light and quite pale in colour. Add the eggs one at a time and beat well between each addition. (If the butter and sugar are not creamed properly and if you add the eggs too fast, the mixture will curdle, resulting in a cake with a heavier texture.) Sieve the flour and baking powder and *stir* in gradually. Mix all together lightly and add 1 tablespoon of milk to moisten.

Divide the mixture evenly between the 2 tins, hollowing it slightly in the centre. Bake for 20–25 minutes or until cooked. Turn out onto a wire tray and allow to cool.

Sandwich together with home-made Raspberry Jam and whipped cream. Sprinkle with sieved castor sugar. Serve on an old-fashioned plate with a doyley.

Ballymaloe Brown Yeast Bread*

When making Ballymaloe Brown Yeast Bread, remember that yeast is a living fungus. In order to grow, it requires warmth, moisture and nourishment. The yeast feeds on the sugar and produces carbon dioxide which makes the bread rise. Hot water will kill yeast. Have the ingredients and equipment at blood heat. The yeast will rise on sugar or treacle. At Ballymaloe we use treacle. The dough rises more rapidly with 110 g/4 ozs yeast than with only 55 g/2 ozs yeast.

The flour we use is stone-ground wholemeal. Different flours produce breads of different textures. The amount of natural moisture in flour varies according to atmospheric conditions. The quantity of water should be altered accordingly. The dough should be just too wet to knead—in fact it does not require kneading. The main ingredients—wholemeal flour, treacle and yeast—are highly nutritious.

For 4 loaves

1.5 kg/3½ lbs/11¼ cups wholemeal flour
1.4 L/2½ pints/50 fl ozs approx. water at blood heat (mix yeast with 290 ml/½ pint/10 fl ozs lukewarm water)

4 loaf tins (13 x 20 cm/5 x 8 inches approx.)

20g/1 tablesp./4 American teasp. salt
1–2 well rounded teasp. black treacle
55–110 g/2–4 ozs/½ –1 cup yeast
sesame seeds (optional)

For 1 loaf

450 g/1 lb/scant 3 cups wholemeal flour
350–425 ml/12–15 fl ozs/1½ –2 scant cups water at blood heat (mix yeast with 150 ml/5 fl ozs/ generous ½ cup lukewarm water approx.)

1 loaf tin (13 x 20 cm/5 x 8 inches approx.)

1 teasp. black treacle
5 g/1 teasp./1 American teasp. salt
30 g/1 oz fresh yeast
sesame seeds (optional)

Preheat the oven to 230°C/450°F/regulo 8.

Mix the flour with the salt and warm it very slightly (in the cool oven of an Aga or Esse, or in a gas or electric oven when starting to heat). In a small bowl, mix the treacle with some of the water (290 ml/$\frac{1}{2}$ pint/10 fl ozs approx. for 4 loaves and 150 ml/5 fl ozs/generous $\frac{1}{2}$ cup for 1 loaf), and crumble in the yeast. Put the bowl in a warm position such as the back of the cooker. Grease bread tins and put them to warm, also warm a clean tea-towel. Look to see if the yeast is rising. It will take 5 minutes approx. to do so and will have a creamy and slightly frothy appearance on top.

When ready, stir it well and pour it, with most of the remaining water, into the flour to make a wettish dough. The mixture should be too wet to knead. Put the mixture into the greased, warmed tins and sprinkle with sesame seeds if you like. Put the tins back in the same position as used previously to raise the yeast. Put the tea-towel over the tins. In 20 minutes approx. the loaves will have risen by twice their original size. Remove the tea-towel and bake the loaves in a hot oven, 230°C/450°F/ regulo 8 for 45–50 minutes, or until they look nicely browned and sound hollow when tapped.

We usually remove the loaves from the tins about 10 minutes before the end of cooking and put them back into the oven to crisp all round, but if you like a softer crust there's no need to do this.

Note: Dried yeast may be used instead of baker's yeast. Follow the same method but use only half the weight as given for fresh yeast. Allow longer to rise.

Ballymaloe Cheese Biscuits

Makes 25–30 biscuits

We serve these biscuits with our Irish farmhouse cheese trolley in the Ballymaloe restaurant. Although we make them fresh every day, they do keep for several weeks in an airtight tin and also freeze well.

110 g/4 ozs/1 cup brown flour	30 g/1 oz/2 tablesp. butter
110 g/4 ozs/1 cup white flour	1 tablesp. cream
$\frac{1}{2}$ teasp. baking powder	water as needed, 5 tablesp.
$\frac{1}{2}$ teasp. salt	approx.

Mix the brown and white flour together and add the salt and baking powder. Rub in the butter and moisten with cream and enough water to make a firm dough.

Roll out to 3 mm/$\frac{1}{8}$ inch thick approx. Prick with a fork. Cut into rounds with a 6.5 cm/2$\frac{1}{2}$ inch round cutter. Bake on an ungreased baking sheet at 150°C/300°F/regulo 2 for 45 minutes approx. or until lightly browned.

Jane's Biscuits

Makes 25 biscuits approx.

These delicious little shortbread biscuits are easy to make and we serve them with fruit fools, compôtes or just with a cup of tea.

170 g/6 ozs/1$\frac{1}{4}$ cups flour   **55 g/2 ozs/$\frac{1}{4}$ cup castor sugar**
110 g/4 ozs/1 stick butter

Sieve the flour and sugar into a bowl and rub in the butter with the fingertips. Within a few minutes the mixture will start to come together, so gather it up and knead it lightly in the bowl. (This is a shortbread so do not use any liquid.)

Roll out to 7 mm/$\frac{1}{4}$ inch thickness on a lightly-floured board. Cut into 6 cm/2$\frac{1}{2}$ inch rounds or into heart shapes. Bake in a moderate oven 180°C/350°F/regulo 4 until pale brown, 15 minutes. Remove and cool on a rack. Dredge lightly with icing or castor sugar.

Raspberry Jam*

Makes 3 × 450 g/1 lb pots

Raspberry Jam is the easiest and quickest of all jams to make, and one of the most delicious.

900 g/2 lbs/8 cups fresh   **900 g/2 lbs/4$\frac{1}{2}$ cups white sugar**
  raspberries

Wash, dry and sterilise the jars in a moderate oven 180°C/350°F/regulo 4 for 15 minutes. Heat the sugar in a moderate oven for 5–10 minutes.

Put the raspberries into a wide stainless steel saucepan and cook for 3–4 minutes until the juice begins to run, then add the hot sugar and stir over a gentle heat until fully dissolved. Increase the heat and boil steadily for about 5 minutes, stirring frequently.

Test for a set by putting about a teaspoon of jam on a cold plate, leaving it for a few minutes in a cool place. It should wrinkle when pressed with a finger. Remove from the heat immediately. Skim and pour into sterilised jam jars. Cover immediately.

Hide the jam in a cool dry place or else put on a shelf in your kitchen so you can feel great every time you look at it! Anyway, it will be so delicious it won't last long!

Loganberry Jam

Makes 6 × 450 g/1 lb pots approx.

Loganberries rarely appear for sale in the shops, so if you have a little space in your garden it would be well worth putting in a couple of canes, particularly of the new thornless varieties.

1.35 kg/3 lbs/12 cups loganberries	**1.35 kg/3 lbs/6$\frac{3}{4}$ cups white sugar**

Wash, dry and sterilise the jars in a moderate oven, 180°C/350°F/regulo 4, for 15 minutes. Heat the sugar in a moderate oven for 5–10 minutes.

Put the loganberries into a wide stainless steel saucepan and cook for 5–6 minutes until the juice begins to run. Then add the hot sugar and stir over a gentle heat until fully dissolved. Increase the heat and boil steadily for about 5 minutes, stirring frequently.

Test for a set by putting about a teaspoon of jam on a cold plate, leaving it for a few minutes in a cool place. It should wrinkle when pressed with a finger. Remove from the heat immediately. Skim and pour into sterilised jam jars. Cover immediately.

Note: If you are short of loganberries you could use half raspberries and half loganberries, and that will also make a delicious jam.

Blackberry and Apple Jam

Makes 9–10 × 450 g/1 lb jars approx.

All over the countryside every year, blackberries rot on the hedge-rows. Think of all the wonderful jam that could be made—so full of Vitamin C! This year organise a blackberry picking expedition and take a picnic. You'll find it's the greatest fun, and when you come home one person could make a few scones while someone else is making the jam. The children could be kept out of mischief and gainfully employed drawing and painting home-made jam labels, with personal messages like 'Lydia's Jam—keep off!', or 'Grandma's Raspberry Jam'. Then you can enjoy the results of your labours with a well-earned cup of tea.

Blackberries are a bit low in pectin, so the apples help it to set as well as adding extra flavour.

2.3 kg/5 lbs/20 cups blackberries **1.625 kg/4½ lbs/10¼ cups sugar**
900 g/2 lbs/8 cups cooking apples
  (Bramley, or Grenadier in
  season)

Wash, peel and core and slice the apples. Stew them until soft with 290 ml/½ pint of water in a stainless steel saucepan; beat to a pulp.

Pick over the blackberries, cook until soft, adding about 145 ml/¼ pint of water if the berries are dry. If you like, push them through a coarse sieve to remove seeds. Put the blackberries into a wide stainless steel saucepan or preserving pan with the apple pulp and the heated sugar, and stir over a gentle heat until the sugar is dissolved.

Boil steadily for about 15 minutes. Skim the jam, test it for a set and pot into warm spotlessly clean jars.

Damson Jam

Makes 4–4.5 kg/9–10 lbs approx.

Damson Jam was always a great favourite of mine as a child. My school friends and I used to collect damsons every year in a field near the old castle in Cullohill. First we ate so many we almost burst—the rest we brought home for Mummy to make into Damson Jam.

2.7 kg/6 lbs damsons **1.290 ml/1½ pints/3¾ cups water**
2.7 kg/6 lbs sugar

Pick over the fruit carefully, wash and drain well and discard any damaged damsons. Put the damsons and water into a greased stainless steel preserving pan and stew them gently until the skin breaks. Heat the sugar in a low oven, add it to the fruit and stir over a gentle heat until the sugar is dissolved. Increase the heat and boil steadily, stirring frequently. Skim off the stones and scum as they rise to the top. Test for a set after 15 minutes boiling. Pour into hot sterilised jars and cover. Store in a cool dry place.

Note: The preserving pan is greased to prevent the fruit from sticking to the bottom.

Notes

Notes

Notes